D1588624

John
Woolman:
CHILD OF LIGHT

John Woolman:

CHILD OF LIGHT

THE STORY OF JOHN WOOLMAN
AND THE FRIENDS

by Catherine Owens Peare

author of "MARY McLEOD BETHUNE," etc.

The Vanguard Press, New York

To the Memory of Charles Gilpin Cook

ACKNOWLEDGMENTS

The author wishes to express sincere thanks to the following for their generous help:

Josephine M. Benton, Philadelphia, Pa.

Tessa Cadbury, Pemberton, New Jersey

Jane B. and Daniel S. Dye, John Woolman Memorial, Mount Holly, New Jersey

Dorothy Lloyd Gilbert, Committee on Preservation of Records, Guilford College, North Carolina

Dorothy G. Harris, Acting Librarian, Friends Historical Library, Swarthmore College, Swarthmore, Pa.

Eleanor N. Melson, Department of Records, Philadelphia Yearly Meeting, Philadelphia, Pa.

The staff of the Grand Army Plaza Branch, Brooklyn Public Library, Brooklyn, N. Y.

Two scholars have left us detailed and competent sources of authentic information on John Woolman: Amelia Mott

Gummere in her book, *The Journal and Essays of John Woolman*; and Janet Whitney in her biography, *John Woolman, American Quaker* (Little, Brown and Company), and in her definitive edition of *The Journal of John Woolman* (Henry Regnery Company). Quotations from John Woolman's *Journal* and his other writings used in this text have been taken chiefly from these sources.

CONTENTS

John
Woolman:
CHILD OF LIGHT

I

ON THE RANCOCAS

The gray, glassy surface of the Rancocas River began to show through the low-hanging mist as the morning sun rose higher. A boy of eight watched its curving, meandering course grow visible. He knew every foot and yard of the Rancocas for miles in both directions and the forests that flanked its farther side. He knew the deer and the beaver, the wild teal and the quail, the Indian trails and the seasons.

John Woolman gazed around him with a solemn face, watching the myriad columns of morning fog rise like the smoke of buried fires from a freshly plowed field. He was sitting on a rise of ground, almost motionless, out of earshot of the farmhouse. He had come out here to get away from the after-breakfast bustle, away from his chattering brothers and sisters.

A faint ripple had developed on the surface of the river.

The ripple was followed by others in rapid succession as the bow of a dugout canoe appeared out of the mist. In it sat a solitary Lenape, bronzed by the weather and naked except for his leather breechclout. His head was shaved to the tufted scalp lock on top, left there as a defiance to his enemies. The canoe glided upriver without a sound and disappeared again into the flatlands fog.

There was no terror for the boy in the sight of an Indian in 1728, because his family and neighbors had been friends with the Indians for generations, since the time his grandfather had first purchased this tract and cleared its surface for cultivation.

What did terrify him was a dream he had had the night before. A long dream! He couldn't remember how long it had lasted, maybe all night; but he had awakened with it still vivid in his memory, still taunting and teasing his quick and fertile imagination. He sat in silence and tried to understand it.

In his dream he had stood in the doorway of his father's house and had watched the moon rise near the west and travel across the sky to the east. When the moon was overhead, a small cloud had drifted down and settled on the ground no more than a hundred feet away. The cloud turned into a beautiful green tree. No sooner had the moon disappeared than the sun began to rise. The intense heat of the sun withered and destroyed the tree. Next, in the garbled way of dreams, a "being" appeared, and his dream's mind told him positively that the "being" was a "sun worm."

What was a sun worm? How could he have known what to call it? Why had the tree died? Why had he dreamed as he had? Was the dream to warn him that he had done something wicked? Was the sun going to wither him for his sins?

Children in John Woolman's time were taught early to

worry about the state of their souls. Life after death was a grave and constant concern with adults, and an almost daily conversation piece. They passed their concern on to their children. Out of it a young imagination could manufacture strange fears and images.

John Woolman closed his eyes and concentrated on wordless prayer, as he had been trained to do, excluding from his consciousness even the early morning songs of the birds. After a brief meditation he opened his eyes again and felt a little more secure.

The heightening sun stirred his conscience and he stood up. This was First Day, (Sunday) the first day in the week, day of rest and of community worship. By now the family must be gathered and preparing to set out. With a sudden burst of speed he raced up the rise of ground from the river and toward the brick farmhouse.

His mother was already mounted on a horse and holding the new infant, Uriah, in her arms. His father was mounted on another horse with two-year-old Hannah before him and four-year-old Abner straddling the rump behind him. The rest of the children—Asher, six; Patience, ten; Sarah, eleven; and Elizabeth, thirteen—were old enough to walk.

As John raced up to the group, his father spoke in a gentle but rebuking tone, "We will be late to Meeting because of thee."

John Woolman took the reprimand into his heart and walked along with his family as they started down the dirt road.

"Where didst thou go?" demanded Elizabeth. "We called and called."

He ignored his sister's question, concentrating on the crunching sound that his heavy shoes made on the pieces of clamshell spread along the road to make it solid.

Last night's dream still bothered him. It wasn't crumbling away and disappearing from memory as dreams sometimes did.

"Hast thou ever seen a sun worm?" he asked Elizabeth. She shook her head.

"A what?" asked Patience.

"A sun worm."

"Ask father. He will know."

John ran to the head of Samuel Woolman's horse and repeated his question. "Hast thou ever seen a sun worm?"

Samuel Woolman looked down at his son with a sober and humorless face.

"I know of no such creature."

The puzzled boy held his peace. Perhaps during Meeting the meaning of his dream would be made clear to him.

The party moved on, past the school where the Woolman children spent their weekdays, until at last they arrived in front of the Quaker Meeting House. That they were late arrivals was apparent enough. There were no dawdlers outside, no friendly handshakes; all had gone in. Other horses stood riderless in the horseshed.

John felt his embarrassment deeply as his parents dismounted and his father led the two horses into the remaining space in the three-sided log shelter. No matter how quiet they tried to be, the entrance of nine heavily shod Woolmans would create a disturbance.

The log building, with its solitary window up behind the elders' seats, its beaten clay floor, and its severely narrow benches, offered little in the way of cheer; but cheer was not its function.

Samuel and Elizabeth Woolman preceded their flock through the door, and each in turn as he stepped inside responded automatically to the deep quiet of the assembled

worshipers, trying to walk noiselessly, slide into a wooden
bench, and become motionless at once. Elizabeth Woolman
and her daughers turned to the left and sat with the women.
Samuel Woolman and his sons sat on the right with the men.

The Friends in their drab garments, the women with neat
caps on their heads, the men wearing hats with round crowns
and moderate brims, sat in rows on the long, comfortless
benches. On the facing seats sat some half dozen of the most
responsible and most respected members of the congregation.
No decoration or imagery distracted their attention. No
minister addressed them. Mystics, they sat with their own
thoughts laid aside, their hearts united, waiting upon the
spirit of God. There would be no sound until one of their
own members, his mind invaded by a spiritual message,
should feel compelled to rise and share his message with the
others.

John Woolman slithered up on the bench with Abner and
Asher, three pairs of feet dangling in space. He saw his father
bow his head for a moment, eyes closed, then lift his head
and look straight ahead. This was a time, John knew, to resolve his problems: his puzzling dream and his discomfort at
having made his family late to Meeting.

The jostling and squirming of his four-year-old brother
distracted him, and he quieted the unfeeling baby with a
sharp elbow. He wanted to concentrate, to shed his burdens
so that the rest of the day could be fair. But the psychic power
of the meeting was too much for a small boy to cope with. It
caught him up and held him and commanded his thinking
into its channel. He belonged to it. He felt the silence close
over him like a deep green sea.

At last, upon a signal from one of the elders, the Meeting
rose, and conversation began in hushed tones at first, gradually
gaining volume, as Quakers turned to one another and clasped

hands in fellowship and addressed one another as "Friend." Not Sir or Madam, not Excellency or Highness, not even Mister; just Friend.

The Friends' use of thee and thou in addressing anyone was a custom they had adopted when the Society was founded in England. It was known as the "plain talk," or talk of the common folk. They refused to use the plural "you" except where the plural was called for, since it was a means of expressing courtesy and deference, especially to those of higher rank. Friends believe that all men are created equal and that none deserves any greater courtesy than any other.

The Woolman children, like the other youngsters, burrowed their way through the congestion of adults and burst upon the out of doors. The sun was high in the sky; the fog had disappeared. No need to wait for their elders on the way home; so down the road they raced, all but John. He walked slowly, running his fingertips among the leaves of the wild shrubs.

Burlington County, like all of West New Jersey, was feeling the influence of fall. The leaves of the sumac were beginning to match its red berries. The goldenrod was in full bloom. The tall, stately maples, changed ahead of the other trees, stood out in brilliant relief against the forest.

John glanced back over his shoulder. His parents would not be along for some time, because the after-meeting comradery would hold them for at least half an hour.

He stepped off the road and once again sat down in the tall grass to think about his dream. He wasn't afraid of it any more. Somehow, his hour of worship, even though it hadn't explained his sun worm, had taken the terror out of it. Perhaps his dream had been the devil tempting him. He felt it had been important in any event, even though he couldn't have explained it to anyone else.

For additional assurance he took out his Bible and turned
to the pages where he knew he would find the most vivid and
colorful language, the Book of Revelation. His halting ability
to read had spelled out the words before: "the tree of life with
its twelve kinds of fruit . . . and the leaves of the trees were
for the healing of the nations. . . ."

Trees, leaves, fruit—all imagery that a farm boy could comprehend, imagery interwoven with imaginative dreaming,
with mysticism, and with a primitive fear of the Almighty.

The dull clip-clop of hoofs traveling the dirt road made
him look up, and he saw the two horses that had borne his
parents to Meeting returning homeward, held to a walk because of the small children they were carrying. When they
came abreast of their other son sitting in the grass, Samuel
and Elizabeth Woolman reined up their mounts.

"What art thou reading?" asked Samuel.

"Scripture," replied the sober-faced boy, holding up the
familiar volume.

His mother smiled at him so contagiously that he could
not help but smile up at her in return.

"Thou must come home, John," she said. "Mount up behind me."

She gathered her long gray cape closer around her as he put
one foot in a stirrup and took hold of the saddle to haul himself up. He could read at home just as well. Worth-while reading on First Day afternoon was encouraged.

There was no further word about the delay John had
caused his family that morning, and he knew there would be
none. As they moved placidly homeward, John Woolman felt
safe and free, his wrong deeds wholly attoned for; and the
feeling of security dissolved his gloomy mood. By the time the
horses reached his own yard, he was ready to race after Asher,
but a firm suggestion from Samuel held him.

"Help thy mother."

Dutifully he stood beside her horse and received the warm, live, moving bundle of infant while she dismounted, eager to give it back to her the instant she stood firmly on the ground.

John Woolman glanced longingly at the river and woods, but even though he had already made his peace with eternity he knew he could not run wild today. There were six other days in the week for that. So he walked quietly into the living room with its wide board floors, hand-woven scatter rugs, its Windsor-backed chairs, and its huge fireplace, where the oldest daughter, Elizabeth, had already hung an iron kettle on its swinging crane to heat over the fire. The table would have to be laid, but John did not have to think about that. That was woman's work. His duties would begin early tomorrow morning before he went to school, gathering the fall crop of apples.

With a deep concern for the value of wholesome learning, every Quaker family leaving that meeting had returned home to its close-knit circle to spend its First Day in a kind of devotional retirement of reading. There was no fiction or other light matter in their libraries that might tend to corrupt, but the Scriptures contained vigorous drama, and there were the writings of such Quakers as George Fox and William Penn that held their own kind of excitement.

George Fox, founder of the Society of Friends, had written a journal of his life and experiences. His electrifying personality had created a whole new movement less than a hundred years before John Woolman's time, and the inspiration lived on in his writings. Fox had been the son of a humble weaver in England and had been apprenticed to a shoemaker, but by the time he was nineteen his deep interest in religion was apparent. None of the existing churches had satisfied him, neither the Church of England, nor the Puritans, nor the Presbyterians, and he had set out as a seeker to wander around the countryside trying to find answers to all the questions that bothered him. He wandered for four years, talking to religious leaders, sitting in the open fields to read his Bible and pray. At last one day the light of understanding came to him. "Then I heard a voice which said, 'There is one, even Christ Jesus, that can speak to thy condition'; and when I heard it, my heart did leap for joy," he wrote in his journal. "Then the Lord let me see why there was none upon the earth that could speak to my condition."

Fox had begun almost at once to preach of his new mystical discovery to others, and a crowd of followers gathered around him—his "Children of Light." They called themselves Friends and were called Quakers in derision because they sometimes quaked and trembled when the spirit of God within them forced them to rise and speak. They endured cruel persecutions and imprisonments for their new faith, just as other sects had in ancient England; for church and government were one, and none dared oppose either without risk. When some of the Quakers emigrated to New England they were persecuted there, too, for differing from the established faith.

William Penn had been a wealthy young man of titled family when he first heard a Quaker preacher. He eventually became "convinced" and joined the Society of Friends, giving up his fancy clothes for the plain attire and becoming a minister and writer of Friends' doctrine of truth, peace, gentleness, and simplicity.

William Penn had created John Woolman's world. He had outlived Fox by a quarter of a century and had died in 1718, only two years before John Woolman was born. Penn worried a great deal about the sufferings of the Friends. When John Berkeley and George Carteret sold the western half of New Jersey to Quakers, William Penn was called in to help divide the land fairly. Penn finally became one of the managers of the land, and the idea occurred to him that here would be a refuge for persecuted Quakers of both England and New England. In West New Jersey the Quakers could escape from whippings, imprisonment, and impoverishment and establish a settlement of their own where they could worship as they pleased.

John Woolman's grandfather, then a young man in his early twenties, was one of the adventuresome group that bought land fronting on the Rancocas River—bought it sight unseen—and arrived when the Quaker colony was first being established. John the elder was not with the first arrivals, but he was among the earliest. He sailed up the Delaware River as far as the village of Burlington, taking shelter with the settlers who had preceded him until he could make his way eastward and build on his own grant of land with its nearly two hundred and fifty yards on the Rancocas Creek and its expanse northward of two miles.

William Penn's influence was deeply felt in the planning of West Jersey colonies, and the success of the Jersey settlements inspired Penn to try a Friends' settlement on a vaster scale. Just a few years later, Penn acquired lands on the other side of the Delaware River and created his "Holy Experiment," Pennsylvania, a whole province where self-governing, fair-dealing, God-fearing folk could dwell together in peace. The Holy Experiment prospered, and so did the Friends of Pennsylvania and New Jersey. The thinking of William Penn spread like a glow over their lives.

John Woolman sat cross-legged on the floor of the house which his grandfather had built, listening as his father read to the family. His grandfather was gone now, but in one corner stood the loom that the first Woolman had brought from England because he had been a weaver by trade. John's father, the second Woolman, still used it to turn out fabrics for the family to wear. The loom was a clumsy, space-consuming device on its four big wooden posts.

The loom, like his mother's spinning wheel, was still on First Day.

"I shall read something from the writings of William Penn," said Samuel Woolman to his family when mealtime had passed.

To John Woolman the pattern was completely familiar; so were the words he would hear.

"In conversation mark well what others say and do, and hide your own mind, at least till last; and then open it as sparingly as the matter will let you. . . . Speak last and little but to the point. . . ."

The boy sat immobile, his attention coming and going as he caught only fragments and snatches.

"Return no answer to anger, unless with much meekness. . . . Be plain in clothes, furniture and food, but clean. . . . The rest is folly and a snare. . . . Love silence, even in the mind; for thoughts are to that as words to the body, trouble-some. . . ."

Their faith was a pattern for daily living, created from the cradle, and the room in which the family gathered gave testi-mony: their unadorned, unupholstered furniture, their sim-ple farm food, the spinning wheel and loom that made their homespun clothing.

As Samuel Woolman read on, the love that ruled their lives, binding them to one another and to their neighbors, gave his restrained voice a rich timbre.

"They that love beyond the world cannot be separated by it. Death cannot kill what never dies."

A CONTRARY DISPOSITION

John Woolman, his three older sisters, and two younger brothers were covering the half mile to school on Second Day morning at a high rate of speed. They wore clothes that were the exact duplicates of those worn by adults, the boys in knee breeches, hand-knit stockings, and buckled, square-toed shoes; the girls in long, full skirts, tight bodices, and aprons tied neatly around their middles. Elizabeth, the oldest and the assistant mother of the brood, whirled round and rebuked them:

"Walk more slowly. Abner is too small to keep up."

It was hard to be moderate in the sharp, bracing October air. John found himself several yards ahead of the others, and he turned around to wait. Watching the breathless, almost running gait of the baby brother whom he had so heartlessly jabbed with his elbow in yesterday's meeting, he was suddenly full of remorse and compassion.

"Walk ahead," he told the others. "I will hold Abner's hand."

He took the small hand in his own and slowed his pace, arriving at the schoolhouse door minutes behind the rest.

School was almost as gentle as home; at least the schoolmaster tried to make it so. His pupils were not whipped or caned according to the prevailing custom of the day. The more severe the whipping the deeper the learning, thought most people, but not the Friends. They made their appeal to the heart and mind, beginning as soon as a child could respond to teaching. Quaker children often started school at the age of four.

The one-room school building, just twenty feet square, had been built even earlier than the Meeting House, nearly forty years before John Woolman's birth, so seriously did Friends regard education. George Fox himself had urged the establishment of schools for teaching boys, and for girls, too, "to instruct lasses and maidens in whatsoever things were civil and useful in the creation."

Near the Rancocas school building was an old spring that the Indians and Friends used together, for an Indian village had once stood on this site.

The Woolmans took their places on the benches with the children from other plantations along the Rancocas River as well as a sprinkling of Lenape children whose parents chose to send them to the Friends' school.

"Learn and teach your children fair writing, and the most useful points of mathematics and some business when young whatever else they are taught," William Penn had written, and his words proved to be a fair definition of their curriculum.

Penmanship was an art in those days, and the Quaker schoolmaster's students were required to devote many pages to practice. Friends' records, kept by those same students who spent tedious hours over their copybooks, are written in round, beautiful script as readable as modern printing. Grammar and geography were considered essential, and to spell correctly was another high-ranking virtue, but mathematics was the highest of all, and it included bookkeeping. Many would become merchants, and they must look after their own affairs intelligently.

John Woolman's handwriting was not so beautiful as some of his contemporaries'; it seemed to be driven uphill by his own intensity; but the characters stood straight and even and well shaped. His fingers grew tighter and tighter around his pencil as he wrote the same sentence again and again or practiced a row of some difficult letter of the alphabet.

"Thou art writing too rapidly," the schoolmaster would say, laying an understanding hand on the boy's head.

It was part of John Woolman's hunger for understanding, a desire to be on with it, to master this step so that he could tackle the next. He was seeking, seeking, seeking to know.

"Patience!" his teacher would counsel, and conscientiously John would force himself to a more moderate pace.

Learning was a continuous thing to his ardent mind. It carried on after school to whatever book he had in his pocket or whatever book he could find in his father's library: travel books by the Jesuit Fathers telling of their explorations in India and Africa, Robert Barclay's *Apology* for the Friends' faith, and the ever-available Fox and Penn.

But the vitality of a growing boy could not be entirely consumed by his reading, however intense his desire for knowledge, nor even by the heavy chores of a farm. A body nourished on game meat, Indian corn, wild honey, home-grown vegetables and fruits, skillfully turned-out breads and pastries, and the milk, butter, and cheese from the Woolmans' own dairy animals could go on almost without ceasing from sunrise to sunset. The country was wild and rough and endless to a boy's perspective, and he could explore on foot or on horseback over miles of Indian trails, visiting in the Lenape wigwams, as much at home in their dome-shaped houses of chestnut or hickory saplings covered with corn leaves and bark as he was in his own.

Sometimes he saw Indians from the hills of Pennsylvania come down the trails and across New Jersey on the way to the coast for fishing expeditions. They would camp for days on the seashore, gathering clams, stringing and smoking them over campfires, carrying them back to Pennsylvania in their hand-woven baskets for winter use. On the shore they left great piles of clamshells that the first European settlers found and used to strengthen their roadways.

The winter deepened, and the deciduous trees lost their leaves; the grass withered, and the ground hardened. Soon the Woolman children were plowing through snow on their way to school, where the primitive fireplace would sear them on one side and leave them chill on the other. The schedule was not made easier because it was winter. School met six days a week, with or without snow.

Winter did shorten the days, though, driving the children indoors before they were ready to go. Then John could watch his father weaving. Or sometimes Samuel Woolman would dip into his law books, for he knew some law, too.

His mother and older sisters usually sat knitting, or one of them took her place at the spinning wheel. The clothes he wore had a long history before they reached the wearable state, and he knew it all, from shearing the fleece from the sheep, teasing it into fluff, carding it between two pieces of wood with wire teeth, to fastening the neat roll onto the distaff or upright pole alongside the spinning wheel so that it could be drawn into thread for his father's loom. Indoor industries lasted until spring came around once more.

Spring stimulated his young boy's vitality to its maximum; it left him flowing over with energies that he could not understand but knew only that they must be spent. It exerted pressures on him that school and field labor and even the rich language of the Book of Revelation could not absorb. It sent him racing and running and climbing and tempted him to feats of violence.

He hung by his hands from the branch of an apple tree and swung back and forth until he had enough momentum to let go, landing several feet ahead. Then he rushed on to the next tree, and to the next and the next, roaming on through the acreage of the next plantation. The sap was up in the branches or they might have cracked under his weight, and showers of pink and white petals fell around him from the blossoms that heralded the apple crop.

He caught sight of a carelessly built nest of grass and mud high on a conspicuous branch and knew at once that it belonged to Burlington County's noisiest clarion of spring: the robin. The bird started up from her nest in alarm as he approached and it darted back and forth shrilling her protest, because she had young in the nest. The robin to the farmer is both a protector and a pest; protector because it consumes so many worms and insects and pest in turn because of its ravenous appetite for ripening fruit. But to John Woolman the robin was a sporting target, and he picked up a supply of stones, shying them one after another at the bird. Any target is a temptation, and a moving target the most challenging of all. One of the stones finally found its mark, and the dead bird plummeted to the ground.

John Woolman rushed on, thoughtless and unheeding, looking for other ways to spend his energy. But long before the sun was set his training had begun to seep up from his subconscious and cloud his carefree happiness. He had killed. He had snuffed out the life of one of God's creatures. There was no way he could undo that now, he reflected, but the young in the nest would also perish because the parent wasn't there to feed them. So, really, he had killed more than one, and only one had died mercifully. The others must starve slowly.

Turning back, he began to retrace his way across the fields to the orchard, hoping that he would be able to remember which tree held the nest. He found it, and taking hold of a lower branch swung himself up and began to climb until he reached the level of the nest. Four wide-open yellow mouths begged for food. He had seen enough husbandry to know that there are times when lower creatures have to die, and he also knew that death must be quick and kindly. He lifted each birdlet from the nest in turn and ended its breathing with a deft thumb and forefinger.

As John Woolman grew older, the conflict between the natural boy and the saint, or deeply religious person he was to become, deepened. There was precious little of real evil in the atmosphere in which he grew up, yet imperfections in his friends and in himself that were only human tortured him to a depth that they could not reach in anyone else. Ill language offended him. As his knowledge and perspective increased from his constant reading, he drew comparisons between men of the past and men of the present. The present didn't always measure up.

"From what I had read and heard I believed there had been, in past ages, people who walked in uprightness before God in a degree exceeding any that I knew or heard of now living; and the apprehension of there being less steadiness and firmness amongst people in the present age often troubled me while I was still a child," he wrote years later.

Yet, up to the time that he was sixteen, the lusty boy had the upper hand and caused the developing saint no end of remorse and self-reproach.

In his twelfth year, as he stood by the road to see his father off to Yearly Meeting, he received his standard admonition: "Remember, thou art the oldest boy. Thy mother depends on thee."

Samuel Woolman would be gone for the better part of a week to the annual gathering of representatives from all the Friends' Meetings in the Jerseys and Pennsylvania, which then included Delaware. Several Meetings belonged to a Monthly Meeting which, as its name implies, met once a month to transact the local business of the members. Several Monthly Meetings met in quarterly session four times a year for the same purpose to serve a larger area, and the Yearly Meeting served the largest area of all. Philadelphia was really the capital of Quakerism in the New World, and alternate Yearly Meetings were held there, but out of consideration for those who had to travel a great distance, every other year the Yearly Meeting convened in Burlington. In 1732 it met in Burlington, seven miles west by north from Rancocas Village.

"I shall return in time for First Day Meeting," Samuel assured his wife and family.

They watched him mount and disappear down the road. He was not a representative this year, but many more went to Yearly Meeting than were representatives. Women did not participate in the business meetings. They held separate Yearly, Quarterly, and Monthly Meetings of their own and concerned themselves with matters of interest to women.

Elizabeth Woolman remained behind this time because her children totaled nine now, the youngest two and four.

Even in the most loving household there is some lurking tendency to anarchy when the top authority is away. John Woolman's responsibilities suddenly seemed less pressing in his father's absence, and with a whoop he was across the field before he could hear his mother say, "John, bring in more logs for the fireplace."

At the end of the day the logs were there, because Asher had carried them in. When Elizabeth Woolman reminded her eldest son of his neglected duty and asked him to take a leather bucket and draw water from the well, she was told, "Asher will do it."

And this time, the growing, unruly boy was so completely master over the saint that regrets did not creep in at all. There was no sudden coming awake at night with an attack of conscience and creeping out of the feather bed and down the stairs to draw the water. John Woolman's heart had "shut itself up in a contrary disposition," and he thought no more about it until his father returned from Yearly Meeting.

Samuel Woolman took an opportunity to walk alone with his son.

"I understand," he began, "that thou behaved amiss toward thy mother."

John needed a moment to search his memory for his wrong deed, and his father helped him.

"While I was abroad, thy mother reproved thee for a misdeed, and thou made her an undutiful reply."

Ashamed, confused, his conscience reawakened, John Woolman hung his head, while his father spoke on and in a voice laden with understanding asked him to try to do better in the future.

More troubled and depressed than he had been by his sun

"Foolish jesting," whispered his conscience, but it was only a whisper, lost in the happy commotion.

He was not hardy enough to commit any really scandalous acts, but he shared the company of those who did and listened to their boastings with a secret little twinge of envy at their blatant courage.

"Backsliding and vanity," his conscience prodded him again, but the vigor of young manhood swept the reproof away.

He was a good fellow among good fellows, and as he grew older his circle of acquaintances increased. Righteous concern receded into the background; he turned less often to the Scriptures for direction, and the less often he turned to them the less often he felt the need.

His duties on the farm increased as he became bigger and stronger, but that was so for all the young men of a farming community. The difference for Woolman was that he was losing his taste for laboring on the land—plowing, harvesting, caring for animals, hauling water, felling great trees, and cutting firewood.

Samuel and Elizabeth Woolman showed their distress plainly, as they watched their oldest son drift into vanities and creaturely interests.

"Dost thou never consider the quiet, wholesome life any more?" his father would ask when he had the opportunity to be alone with him.

"Thy life is best for thee," John would explain, and tried to make his father understand the appeal that city life held for him, the deep need he felt for gay friends.

Or his mother would look at him anxiously and ask, "John, wilt thou come to Meeting with us?"

Of course, he was coming to Meeting. In a community that was almost entirely Quaker everyone went to Meeting on First Day morning. Their whole life flowered out of the Meeting.

His parents' concern was never wholly lost. There was always something within him that could be stirred to life by their compassion and patience and obvious distress, but whatever they stirred to life lapsed back into quiet almost immediately, to be awakened during the hour of worship, then lost again.

Even the Quaker patterns themselves drew him toward Burlington, because the Monthly, Quarterly, and Yearly Meetings that were held there convened in a meetinghouse that was more sophisticated than the one in Rancocas. Woolman's own grandfather had contributed funds to its construction. It was of brick, with a roof of cedar shingles. Inside, the benches were hewn and polished, the walls were wainscoted head high, and the floors were of wide pine boards.

The lure of secular books was stronger in Burlington, because so many well-to-do Friends living there had sumptuous homes and ample libraries. Burlington was a vital center of West New Jersey; it was a port where seagoing ships came in from Europe bringing news and books along with their merchandise and carrying away the produce of the Jersey farmlands. There was industry in Burlington, too. Thomas Olive, who had been a member of William Penn's commission to purchase the land from the Indians, and whose descendants still lived in Burlington, had built the first mill in the country for grinding corn and grain. And brickyards and pottery works had been there long before John Woolman's time.

The road to Burlington from Rancocas was a well-traveled route, and the logical course for a young man was from country to city.

John Woolman was running a race with God, a swift race, and in his teens John Woolman was way ahead. His circle of acquaintances increased; his knowledge grew as he continued to consume books and periodicals sent to his friends from different parts of the world. In occasional moments of subtle uneasiness he would turn to the Scriptures for comfort and find nothing that satisfied him. Their value was removed from him. His heart and mind had turned away and had "no resolution to return."

Striding along the familiar road to his home one cold, damp day, with large snowflakes wetting his face and melting on his leather jacket, his vision suddenly blurred. His clothing felt too heavy and too tight, and he unbuttoned his jacket around his neck. He was hot, his pulse raced, and he had to slow his pace to keep his balance. He finally reached the door and leaned a hand on the frame to steady himself. As he stepped into the room, Elizabeth, sitting at the flax wheel, took one look at his flushed face and jumped up to help him to a chair.

"Thou art ill!"

She removed his hat and laid a hand on his forehead.

"It is the fever."

Of all his brothers and sisters—and by now there were eleven besides himself, six girls and five boys—Elizabeth was closest to him. Within a month of being five years his senior, she was old enough to be turned to as an adult and yet young enough to understand his point of view when he came into conflict with the adult world. Elizabeth was twenty-two, and she had already assumed much of the responsibility of running the household while her mother turned her attentions to the infant Abraham, two-year-old Rachel, four-year-old Jonah, and seven-year-old Esther.

Seventeen-year-old John seemed much younger to Eliza-

beth than he really was, as he leaned back and closed his
eyes.

"Thou belongest in bed," she said softly, and he yielded
to her direction as she led him up the narrow wooden staircase to the unheated second floor and the small, low-ceilinged
bedroom that he shared with Asher and Abner.

He sank down into the bed, his head throbbing, his joints
aching, while somehow from the outside hands tended him.

"John must sleep alone," he heard his sister say as she bun-
dled everyone off to double up somewhere else.

His mind overstimulated with fever, his imagination confused and garbled, the old conflict between good and evil
came to the surface once more to torture him, and he seemed
to himself, lying there, to be a most piteous creature. Better
never to have been born than to have to suffer these torments.
Better to die now before his wickedness could grow worse.

As his sickness subsided and left him weak but clear in his
mind, he sat propped up against pillows and reflected upon
the state of his soul. A real contrition crept into his heart.
He'd been rebellious against God, he knew now. God was
calling him, calling him to a life of devotion, and he had
been ignoring the call.

As Elizabeth sat by his bedside he took her into his confidence.

"If God pleases to restore my health," he told her, "I shall
serve Him faithfully."

"Thou art already restored," she assured him, and she
smiled at the fortunate results of John's sickness, because she
shared the family's concern for its erring member.

Next to John himself, Elizabeth was the most devout of the
Woolman children. If she had suffered through any indeci-
sions during her adolescence, John would have been too
young to notice. By now she was steady and comforting, a

trustworthy confidante, a capable young woman who was so independent that she was learning the trade of tailoring.

"Wouldst thou like a drink of cool water?" she asked her brother.

"No; I thank thee. The fever has left."

When he finally made the unsteady journey down the stairs and sat by the fireplace with a robe around him, he could see the relieved happiness in the faces of his parents. They said no more about his waywardness, but it was apparent that Elizabeth had given them some encouraging report of his repentance and his return to divine literature.

His strength bounded back once the ailment had left him, and soon he was out of doors, walking around, strolling down the dirt lane toward town, and at last strong enough to cover the five miles to Mount Holly. There were not many directions in which a person could drift in a town with only one real street, and as he stepped over the threshold of the tavern joyous male voices greeted him, warmth overwhelmed him, and he was drawn back into the fellowship of laughter.

The conflict in his soul was sore and intense from then on.

"Thus time passed on; my heart was replenished with mirth and wantonness, while pleasing scenes of vanity were presented to my imagination. . . . I was often sad, and longed to be delivered from those vanities; then again my heart was strongly inclined to them, and there was in me a sore conflict. At times I turned to folly, and then again sorrow and confusion took hold of me."

He yearned as strongly for his Friends' patterns as he yearned to escape them. He sat down in his Meeting for Worship as eagerly as he walked into the tavern, perpetually seeking for the substance that he needed most. His hand reached for books by Quaker authors as expectantly as it reached for worldly information. Somewhere in all of this printed matter must be something that would enlighten him.

Through months of trouble and disquiet he went on seeking the answer to the riddle of himself. Returning from a day spent "wantonly" in Mount Holly or Burlington, he would retire to bed, pick up the Bible that lay on the window sill, and open it at random. He was startled one night by a phrase which caught his glance:

"We lie down in our shame and our confusion covereth us."

The words stood out on the page, vivid, illuminated, revealing John Woolman to himself. He closed the volume and lay back, grateful for the sudden clarity that he felt. Confusion had covered him, and the confusion was being gradually cleared away. If he kept on with his seeking and searching, he would surely find the direction that he must take. If he prayed and waited for guidance, if he was patient enough, if he tried not to yield so easily to foolish things. . . .

He shut his eyes and concentrated all of his attention on God. He withdrew his thoughts from his surroundings and held them in discipline, leaving his mind clear, even slowing his breathing as he brought every nerve and every ounce of awareness to a single focus. Gradually a deep calm stole over him. He drove his attention deeper and deeper into the spiritual awareness that held him, until he felt suspended, lifted, freed of all doubt and confusion. In a kind of bliss, he drifted off to sleep.

The race is not always to the swift. The lusty, carefree, fun-loving boy who had been way out in front was losing ground as his inevitable vocation pursued him.

Foolish things are not so easily or abruptly cast off, though. It was hard to surrender the friendships and companionships upon which he had learned to depend, hard not to walk either toward Mount Holly or Burlington. But he had begun to catch the feel of his direction, and he turned to his Quaker writers with a sense of encouragement, no longer wondering whether he would find the answers he sought but knowing that he ultimately would.

He never went abroad without a volume in his pocket of Penn, Fox, Barclay, Burrough, or the many other "publishers of Truth." He strolled along the roadside, or sat in a field as he had done in childhood, or walked in solitude through the woodland footpaths made by the Indians—thinking, reading, hoping.

It was on one of those solitary walks that he found himself. He had spent the evening indoors reading a pious author, and he had achieved a mood of deep solemnity and humility. Treasuring the mood, he stepped out of the crowded house to which a thirteenth baby had just been added and strolled down the hill toward the Rancocas River. Faint stars showed in the sky, and the night was still except for the murmur of wildlife in the forest.

John Woolman sat upon a fallen log and bowed his head, folding his hands together and pressing them against his forehead. He began to pray—for guidance, for forgiveness, for strength, for courage, for true peace. When the prayer was done, he sat without moving for a long time. He felt the peace increasing within himself; he felt new strength and courage; he felt himself absolved. When he finally rose to return to his room, he understood the guidance he had received. His must be the godly way. He could not run with the pack and find any lasting happiness in it. Gaiety was not for him. He must accept the life of devotion, and—who could tell?—perhaps some day even the ministry.

His personality grew from then on, and his family watched

happily as the gangling, careless boy matured into a dignified young man. He began to seem genuinely happy as he discovered his own community, as he shed his old friends and made new.

He himself moved in a kind of excited expectancy, as each Sunday, or First Day, he strode eagerly into the Meeting for Worship and sat down in the vital silence.

4

NEW FRIENDS FOR OLD

He took new interest in weekday business meetings and felt concern for the affairs of the Society. He joined with his brothers and father with a refreshed zeal in journeying to Monthly and Quarterly Meetings at Burlington and Yearly Meetings at Burlington or Philadelphia. He had been through all of these motions many times before; only now they had new meaning because they held the secret to his future.

Before his increasing seriousness the worthless companions of his youth withdrew and disappeared into the mists of memory. The frequenters of the tavern were lost as soon as he ceased to inhabit their atmosphere.

Influential, or "weighty," Quakers—the Logans, the Pembertons, the Smiths—early felt the impact of John Woolman's developing personality, felt themselves attracted to him, with reservations at first, because they could not be sure that he would not revert, but with growing trust over the long term when they caught flashes and glimpses of his new vision.

There was a gap in John Woolman's social life, when the old friends had dropped away and before the new intimacies had been found. A young man growing up in a large family, blessed with love and affection during all of his formative years, could not help but possess a deep warmth himself to which others would respond; and so the gap was short-lived.

One of the earliest friendships that he made, and one of the closest and most enduring, was with Peter Andrews. Some thirteen years older than John, Peter Andrews was already established in the main current of Society life when John Woolman's interest began to awaken. Peter Andrews appeared frequently in the minutes of Burlington Monthly Meeting as serving on committees or as representative to Quarterly Meeting. John Woolman began to be appointed to committees himself, and he and Peter Andrews were drawn into their close friendship as they worked together.

In 1739, when John Woolman was only nineteen, he was chosen, along with Peter Andrews and others, to represent his Monthly Meeting at the next Quarterly Meeting. It was a step up, a touch of recognition, just the encouragement the young man needed. His father's prestige in the Society could not have done it for him if John had not shown any personal worthiness, but Samuel Woolman did sit back with a frank smile of pride as he watched his oldest son move in the direction for which he had been trained. After the rise of the Meeting Samuel went outside quickly to find his wife and tell her the good news, and for a moment the staid Quaker couple allowed themselves the secret little joy of holding hands.

Elizabeth and Samuel Woolman had declared their intent

to marry in this same Monthly Meeting, and now their sons and daughters were growing up and becoming part of its life.

They turned as John hurried to them.

"Thou hast heard?" he asked his father happily.

Both Elizabeth and Samuel nodded, and seventeen-year-old Asher rushed up to them enthusiastically.

"John is to be a representative to Quarterly Meeting," he announced, as though his parents had just arrived in Burlington.

"I was present," Samuel Woolman reminded him.

"Hast thou told Mother?"

"Thy mother knows."

"I am glad I am not a woman attending the women's business meeting," Asher blurted out tactlessly. "All the important things happen in the men's meeting."

John Woolman turned away from his family to look for Peter Andrews.

"Ask Peter and Esther to come home with us," Elizabeth called after him.

Peter and his wife lived in Mount Holly, and on the way back from Burlington they could partake of the hospitality of the Woolmans. John was grateful for that, because it would give him and Peter more time to talk about concerns to be taken up at next Quarterly Meeting.

There was the problem of spirituous liquors, particularly the sale of rum to the Indians, brought up for discussion again and again. The Friends had come to the Delaware Valley and treated the Indians fairly; other Europeans came to the New World and exploited the Indians mercilessly, buying their lands and furs with baubles, giving them rum to drink so that in their drunkenness they would sell more cheaply. Such exploitation had been going on a long time before Woolman began to think about it. The Lenapes were impoverished by 1740, gradually inched back off their hunting lands; many had become itinerant peddlers of baskets and brooms, or simply beggars, unable to adjust their forest-roving, wild-animal-hunting spirits to agriculture.

Warfare was another problem that disturbed the Friends often in the century before the American Revolution. There were four intercolonial wars in all; two occurred before John Woolman's time; symptoms of the third, which was the result of the rivalry between England and Spain, gathered on the political landscape about the time that John Woolman was beginning to take an interest in the serious concerns of Friends. In Europe it was called the War of the Austrian Succession. In America it was called King George's War, or the War of Jenkins' Ear, because a sea captain named Jenkins claimed that his ear had been cut off by Spanish coast guards. In the New World the third intercolonial war was fought chiefly in the South, between English Georgia and Spanish Florida, and between the English and Spanish navies in the Caribbean. It didn't touch life in Pennsylvania and New Jersey very closely, except when England asked her colonies to raise troops. Since Friends did not believe in any kind of violence or armed conflict, they would have to discuss the rightness or wrongness of serving in the armed forces.

And slavery was another question that had been bothering Friends for more than half a century.

A weighty Quaker stopped John Woolman before he left the Meeting House grounds and complimented him, "I am glad thou art to be a representative to Quarterly Meeting."

"I thank thee, Uncle Joseph."

Joseph Burr was Elizabeth Woolman's brother and lived at Peachfields, the great stone house just two miles north of Mount Holly.

This day there was a visitor with the Burrs, a girl about John's age, who stood demurely aside until Joseph Burr identified her.

"This is Sarah Ellis, my wife's niece," he explained after he had presented John and Sarah to each other. "Her mother has died and she has come from Shrewsbury Monthly Meeting to live with us."

Quakers took care of their own; they had from the earliest days—sheltering those whose lands and goods had been seized by the English government, nursing back to health those who had been hurt by imprisonment or violence, providing for widows, orphans, or other dependents.

"It is nice to have thee with us, Cousin; I am often at Peachfields," said John, clasping hands with her after the manner of Friends; but his head was too full of brand new high purposes to notice Sarah Ellis beyond the fact that she was simply another addition to the Burr household. As soon as he could make a courteous departure he went on in search of Peter Andrews.

Quarterly Meeting would choose representatives to Yearly Meeting; and while John Woolman had no thought of being a representative to Yearly Meeting, since that was an honor reserved for weighty Friends, he would feel an intimate closeness with those who did choose the representatives. He would feel a fraternity with them in everything they discussed and in every decision they made. He would be finding more new associates, more new friends to replace those he had lost.

To each meeting of whatever jurisdiction that John Woolman went he brought an ever-increasing wealth of reading and meditation. His horizons were becoming clearer and sharper; he was growing stronger within himself.

"I kept steady to Meetings, spent afternoons on First Days

in reading the Scriptures and other good books and was early convinced in my mind that true religion consisted in an inward life wherein the heart doth reverence God the Creator and learns to exercise equal justice and goodness not only towards all men but also towards all God's creatures."

He delved into other religions as he read, and found deep similarities.

"I found no narrowness respecting any sects as believing sincere and upright-hearted people in every society who truly loved God were accepted of Him."

Yearly Meeting in 1740 was held in Burlington, while the weather was still fair and after the crops would allow the Quaker farmers to leave their lands for the better part of a week—in September, or Seventh month, as it was called then, because the calendar had not yet been revised and March was the first month of the year.

There the new John Woolman saw old familiar faces that were suddenly possessed of new value, and he and they were drawn to one another by their now mutual convictions.

Anthony Benezet was one of his new associates. A refugee from religious persecutions in France, Anthony Benezet lived in Philadelphia and taught school in nearby Germantown. He was only seven years John Woolman's senior, and already prominent in the Society because of his deep convictions and willingness to give of his time and effort. John Woolman saw in Anthony Benezet's face something of the faith that corresponded to the ardor of his own heart, and the two men became friends almost at once.

There was Thomas Chalkley, elderly minister who for years had devoted most of his time to traveling among the Meetings. He had made the dangerous and difficult ocean crossing between England and the colonies many times in past years, and Meetings for Worship in Trenton, Philadelphia, Burlington, Mount Holly, and Salem knew him well and looked forward to his messages. By the time he reached this Yearly Meeting he had already traveled over five hundred miles through the colonies; but he remained longer in Burlington than he had planned, because on the way his horse had thrown him, badly injuring his hip and shoulder. Traveling Friends seldom allowed physical difficulties to stop them from pursuing their divinely appointed missions. Thomas Chalkley, injuries and all, attended Yearly Meeting and sat in pain and discomfort on the hard, narrow benches. "In the sense of the Love and Goodness of God, and Grace of our Lord Jesus Christ, I was, with many others, much comforted in spirit," was the view that he took of the situation.

John Woolman's view of the situation was that of the young man thrilled by it all, as he listened to the discussions day after day, led and guided by the best Quaker minds from all over Pennsylvania, New Jersey, and Delaware. One by one the Friends' concerns on spirituous liquors, war, slavery, worldliness began to take root in his conscious thinking.

He and Peter Andrews strolled about together during a recess, and he confided to Peter his newly awakened thoughts about slavery.

"Hast thou read Benjamin Lay's essay on slave keeping?" Peter asked him.

Young Woolman shook his head.

"I have a copy that I will give thee."

Peter Andrews did as he promised, but John Woolman did not immediately read the essay after his return to the farm on the Rancocas River, because another event completely diverted his attention. A shopkeeper in Mount Holly offered him an opportunity to escape from farm life, to act as his bookkeeper and tend his shop, living on the premises. John Woolman hurried to his father with the news.

The elder Woolman might have dissuaded the tavern-haunting son from living in Mount Holly without family supervision and influence, but after a long conversation with the newly developing John he gave his nod of approval.

"I really have no taste for farm life," John had explained earnestly on more than one occasion.

John was not the first of the Woolman brood to leave the homestead. Sarah and Patience were both married and running households of their own; and Elizabeth, John's beloved confidante and favorite, had removed herself to the nearby village of Haddonfield to earn her living as a tailor.

He would not be far from Elizabeth in Mount Holly. She would not be lost to him. There was a road running directly from Mount Holly to Haddonfield that was part of an old Indian trail across Jersey from the Delaware River to Shrewsbury on the Atlantic coast. A few hours' horseback ride would bring him to Elizabeth's door, and there he could share his religious experiences with her as of old. Secretly, he knew, it would not be too hard to leave home with Elizabeth already gone.

And in Mount Holly he would find Peter Andrews and would even be able to attend the same Meeting for Worship with him.

The shop where he took up his residence and work stood on the old familiar Mill Street, hugging the sidewalk with its prim front, offering bakery goods, groceries, spices, and such items as a housewife might need: yard goods, thread, needles, buttons. The shop windows looked out on familiar haunts: the tavern that had once caused him so much distress, other shops—harness maker, cobbler, wheelwright. On nearby Pine Street there was an ironworks that turned out handwrought nails, iron plows, and harrows.

John Woolman, because of his exceptionally good education and his absolute honesty, had full responsibility for the shop. His employer lived several miles away, and John Woolman could advise him of the needs of his customers, serve his customers, keep his books of account, and to all intents and purposes be complete master of the little domain.

In the evening, after the shop closed, he could retire to the second floor and his own quarters, there to read and read and read, digging more deeply into the Scriptures, into William Penn, Robert Barclay, and George Fox. No more weariness from exhausting farm labors and no more household hubbub. The solitude he had often craved at home was to be all his now. He could at last, through an amazing number of hours—unbusy moments during the day and all evening—close his eyes and invoke Divine companionship. Here he could hope and wait for his increasing purpose in life to be revealed to him more clearly.

But during the first few nights in that building alone, without the nearness of his family, with not a sound in the street outside, his vivid imagination took hold of him again, and he lay wide awake staring at the shadows in the room and listening intently for distant sounds in the night. Then indeed did he have to call into play all his powers of self-discipline, all his brand new and still untested faith, until he could marshal himself into end-of-the-day prayers and escape into sleep.

While he was still adjusting himself to his new pattern of living, some of his former tavern friends dropped around to renew old acquaintances. They had simply not seen John Woolman for a long time and did not realize the great change that he had experienced.

"I was visited by several young people of my former acquaintance who knew not but vanities would be as agreeable to me now as ever."

They crowded into the little shop, and for a moment their old vitality filled the room. What was he doing now? Did he plan always to be a shopkeeper? Why had they not seen more of him lately? And surely he was going to join them at the end of each working day.

He was sorely tempted out of pure lonesomeness; and for a moment he gave no answer. He felt awfully young, helpless, adrift, until he could give them a weak answer in a faint voice:

"I do not wish to join you."

They laughed! They would have none of it! He was their boon companion. And they could not know as keenly as Woolman did himself how uncertain he felt, his feet resting in the quicksands of indecision.

But the saint was much stronger than the boy by this time, and he was able to exchange banter with his former companions without yielding to them. When the end of the day came and he could at last bolt the door and withdraw to his upstairs quarters, he understood the real value of his solitude. There was no one but himself and God to discuss this, his first real trial.

"I felt myself very weak," he admitted candidly. "At these times, I looked to the Lord for help."

More trials followed, because his day was full of people.

A few months later his master purchased several Scotsmen, indentured servants, from a vessel recently arrived from Europe, and brought them to his shop in Mount Holly until they could be assigned to new masters.

They were big, rough, uncouth fellows, full of common talk, anxious to be on with the business so that they could begin to work out their indentures. The bookish, gentle John Woolman, called upon to supervise them, execute their bills of sale and contracts, was often alone with the rowdy crowd. As he gradually sold them, he reflected that he would be glad when the noise and commotion were done. Until these fellows were through clamoring all day and sleeping short hours of the night, some even having to be accommodated in Woolman's own chamber, there could be no peace.

Gradually the number was whittled down to the last man, who could not be sold because he had taken sick and lay in Woolman's bedroom feverish and delirious.

To be a Friend meant to be a friend to man, any man, and no doubt arose in John Woolman's mind as to his responsibility to the stricken servant. Carefully he nursed him and cared for him and tried his best to restore him to health, as the man lay there cursing and swearing volubly. Woolman's efforts were to no avail, for the man failed rapidly and soon succumbed to his illness.

After the dead man had been carried away, his oaths and curses echoed through John Woolman's memory. His intelligence assured him that the blasphemy of a sick and delirious man could not possibly be effective or significant; yet he was going to have to sleep in the same chamber in which the man had died. Night came inevitably, and John Woolman's candle burned low and at last had to be blown out. The old timorousness returned to embarrass him as shadows and black phantoms stalked the room and eerie distant murmurings imitated the curses that had been hurled against him.

He could get up and go to Peter Andrews' house, or Peter Andrews would gladly come and spend the night with him there. No; he did not have the right to impose on his friends for a mere feebleness in his own nature. In time of real sickness they would come to him automatically. He drew the covers up to his chin and his common sense asserted itself. He had not harmed the man, had not been responsible for his illness or death, nor even for his servitude.

Tomorrow's daylight is always reassuring. When John Woolman awoke he felt a new confidence. These trials in which he won over his own weaknesses were exciting. He was traveling forward; his spirit was growing. Each episode, each decision, was a steppingstone toward a goal that was still too far ahead of him to be visible.

Come First Day he could join Peter Andrews and others in Meeting for Worship in the Mount Holly Meeting House out on Centerton Road at the end of Woodpecker Lane. Traveling that road afoot or on horseback he could see the mount of holly, the only noticeable rise of ground in all that flat country, where giant holly trees grew, giving the town its name.

In Mount Holly Meeting John Woolman had never been a child, and he could feel more the man among men. His father was not there to outrank him, and his younger brothers were not there to reduce him to their age level. As he sat still in the hour of stillness each First Day, his mystical capacities matured, until the morning came when he himself felt the deep compulsion to rise in place and speak.

The words came haltingly out of a parched throat; he almost lost his train of thought completely at the shock of finding himself speaking; then, recapturing his idea and his courage, he shared the worshipful thought that had entered his mind. Vanity did creep in—the unseasoned vanity of being young and being an adult for the first time—and he spoke on beyond the limits of his true message.

"But not keeping close to the true opener, I said more than He directed me to say."

Suddenly sensible of his error, the vanity fell away and

took his self-confidence with it, and he sat down covered with humiliation.

Subsequent prayer and other messages that followed that morning had some healing effect, but it was many weeks before he could dare to speak in Meeting again. Gradually he began to realize that he was at last becoming schooled enough to be a medium for the Divine Word. The saint was increasing as the man emerged. The realization increased his humility to the point where he could at last rise once more, feeling calm and quiet and blessed, say his few words, and find peace in them himself.

"My understanding became more strengthened to know the language of the pure Spirit which moves upon the intellectual deep, and to wait in silence sometimes many weeks together, until I felt that rise which prepares the creature to stand like a trumpet through which the Lord speaks to his people."

John Woolman's was becoming a true ministry.

5

THE GREAT DECISION

The seasons rolled around once more until it was almost time for another Yearly Meeting, this fall in Philadelphia. Interest in Yearly Meeting began to rise weeks, even months, ahead of the event. Yearly Meeting was an occasion for the reunion with distant loved ones, for hearing the Society's most gifted ministers, for exchanging ideas and being brought up to date on the most important questions of the day. It was a time, too, for inward renewal and replenishment of faith.

Planning to travel from Mount Holly or Rancocas to Philadelphia was no small matter. The horseback ride to Cooper's Ferry (now Camden) could be accomplished in a day by a man traveling alone, but when a whole family was journeying to Yearly Meeting and the comfort of women and children had to be considered, it was wiser to spend two days on the trip, stopping overnight at Moore's Inn in Chestertown (now

Moorestown), proceeding on to the Delaware River the next day to take a boat over to Philadelphia.

Philadelphia, planned and laid out by William Penn, was the second largest city in the colonies in 1741, with nearly thirteen thousand residents, about a fourth of whom were Friends. Only Boston was larger. Philadelphia's face to the Delaware was graced by great loading wharves for vessels of trade between the colonies and Europe. Many of those vessels were owned by prosperous Philadelphia Friends, many more were used by Quaker importers and exporters.

Philadelphia, a city of red-brick, white-trimmed Georgian houses, was proud and sensitive of its lovely architecture. The building in which the Pennsylvania Assembly met on Chestnut Street between Fifth and Sixth Streets (now Independence Hall) had an interior graced with fine carvings and sweeping staircases. Philadelphia had brick walks for its pedestrians before they appeared anywhere else in the colonies, with cartways of stone, and the streets slanted to let water drain down the center. By John Woolman's time Philadelphia even had some underground disposal drains.

John Woolman had seen Philadelphia before, but not since his new religious experiences had begun. He and Peter Andrews strolled about town while they waited for the sessions to open. They turned from wealthy Front Street, where the cream of Philadelphia society lived, into High Street (now Market), walking away from the Delaware River, passing the endless procession of shop windows that offered imported wines and spices, ready-made clothing, bolts of silks and cambrics and Irish linens, fine silver plate, precious gems. Philadelphia had everything that the finest European city could offer. No wonder the city-dwelling Quakers were drifting away from their traditional plainness! No wonder their homes were so sumptuous, with finely polished mahogany furniture, silken drapes, and rugs. Creaturely stuff was all around them to tempt their prosperous pocketbooks.

These were the descendants of the Friends who had suffered such privations and persecutions in England; yet their very faith seemed to be their undoing, because their rigid honesty and dependability brought them business and made them rich. Riches, in turn, seemed to draw them away from Quaker plainness.

As young Woolman and Andrews approached the Meeting House they could see other Friends converging on the same location. As they drew closer they became aware of a commotion in the street before the building. They broke into a run and reached the spot just as a rasping voice shouted the words:

"Keepers of slaves! Partakers of the fruits of slave labor!"

"Oh, it is Benjamin Lay!" said Andrews, as he and Woolman worked their way toward the front of the gathering to have a look at the little eccentric.

Lay stood teetering on the edge of the curb on his spindle legs, haranguing the group of Friends right outside their own Meeting House on the sin of enslaving their brothers. Aging Benjamin Lay was no taller than a child, pigeon-breasted, his back badly hunched, his hind quarters shrunken and shriveled; and he was dressed in breeches and knee-length coat of undyed fabric that he had spun and woven himself.

"He dresses that way because dyes are made by slaves," Peter Andrews told John Woolman. "He even eats nothing but milk and such vegetables as he can produce himself."

John Woolman stood and stared at the shocking scene, at the expressions of amusement on the faces of some of the Friends, at the terrible earnestness of the dwarf, as Friends paused for a moment and then passed on into the Meeting. He went in himself and sat down, striving for an inner silence, trying to drive all words from his thinking. But the words would not be dismissed. "Keepers of slaves! Partakers of the fruits of slave labor!" Woolman made a further effort to concentrate to little avail. "Keepers of slaves! Keepers of slaves! Keepers of slaves!" He heard the penetrating voice repeating again and again, as though the ugly little man with his too large head drawn down between too large shoulders had come in to Meeting with him and sat at his side whispering the words into his ear.

The short period of silence that preceded the business meeting ended, and John Woolman was almost relieved when he could give up the struggle and participate in the discussions that were to follow. As soon as he returned to his shop in Mount Holly he must hunt out that article on slave keeping by Benjamin Lay, the one Peter Andrews had given him and he had forgotton in the rush of other matters.

During the several days of sessions he listened with quickened gravity to the topics of the day that were related to the concerns of the Society of Friends. The Assembly of Pennsylvania was Quaker dominated, and so there were times when it was impossible to draw a sharp line between religious and political questions. With war in full swing between England and Spain and with France teetering on the edge, the American colonies were gradually being drawn in.

New Jersey was a crown colony during John Woolman's lifetime, under the direct rule of the King and Parliament of England. Pennsylvania was ruled by proprietary governors but was indirectly under the English crown. In both colonies the large Quaker populations, with their deeply pacifist views, created delicate problems whenever the question of raising troops or levying war taxes came up.

England was rising in the world as a sea power. Her great sailing ships were increasing in number and grandeur. She needed the timber of America for their tall masts and sturdy frames and the pitch and tar that came from southern pines. So England was jealous and wary of any other nation that threatened her colonies. There was France all up through the Mississippi Valley and the St. Lawrence country of Canada. There was Spain in Florida and Mexico and the Caribbean.

It was hard for a young man who had never traveled beyond Philadelphia to comprehend the gravity of these political questions, especially when he had so many problems within himself yet to be solved. Conflicts between the British and French involved the New England colonies; conflicts with the Spanish involved the southern colonies; New Jersey had little military value at that point.

John Woolman returned from Yearly Meeting to his shopkeeping in Mount Holly still troubled by the antic performance of Benjamin Lay. He hunted out the pamphlet Peter Andrews had given him and sat down and read it. In the eighteenth century a book could often have a title a page long, and the title of Lay's pamphlet was:

All slave keepers, that keep the innocent in bondage, apostates. Pretending to lay claim to the pure and holy Christian religion, of what congregation soever, but especially in their ministers, by whose example the filthy leprosy and apostacy is spread far and near; it is a notorious sin which many of the true friends of Christ and his pure truth, called Quakers, have been for many years, and still are, concerned to write and bear testimony against; as a practice so gross and hurtful to religion and destructive to government, beyond what words can set forth, or can be declared of by men or angels, and yet lived in by ministers, and magistrates in America.

It was not a well-composed piece, because it had been written in haste and passion. Benjamin Franklin, who had printed it for Lay, had done his best to make it readable. The pages had not even been in correct order when Lay handed them to him.

"Print any part that thou pleasest first," was Lay's instruction to Franklin.

Woolman was no more concerned with literary merit than Lay had been. He read the explosive, emotional piece through its jerking paragraphs that spoke so penetratingly and so directly to the issue. There was no doubt in Benjamin Lay's mind that to hold a fellow human being in bondage was a woefully unchristian practice.

Putting the pamphlet down, John Woolman sat a long time lost in thought. So many of his friends owned slaves, even his Uncle Joseph. Slaves who belonged to Friends did not fare badly: they were not overworked; they were taught a little and given religious guidance. Benjamin Lay's attitude did seem a little intolerant. Slaves seemed somehow creatures apart, not quite the same, not quite real.

He went about his work in the shop struggling with the new distraction, trying to pay conscientious attention to his responsibilities. The shop was prospering under his devoted care, and his employer had by this time moved into a house right in Mount Holly. Woolman no longer had to sleep in the shop alone but boarded with his master.

At the end of the day Woolman locked up the shop after the last customer and walked homeward to his new residence. He could hardly have been called a boarder, because his own loving and gentle disposition and thoughtfulness had made him almost a member of the family. As he stepped inside the door a plump, mahogany-colored woman bustled forward to help him out of his heavy coat. Her adoration for this righteous young man was entirely frank, and his home-coming, when she could minister to his needs, perhaps even have a chat with him before he retired, seemed to be the high point of her day.

"Good evening," said Woolman, and she responded with a wide-mouthed smile.

He and the family sat down almost immediately to dinner, and after the meal had been cleared away and the Negro woman had retired to the kitchen, the head of the house said casually to Woolman:

"I am planning to sell her. So when you go to the shop to-morrow morning, please draw up a bill of sale."

Sell her? Sell *her*? She was a person, a part of his own life, a friend and companion, someone to whom he told Bible stories and to whom he sometimes confided his minor problems.

When at last he went to his room for the night and closed the door, the memory of a rasping voice flashed through his memory: "Keepers of slaves! Partakers of the fruits of slave labor!" This Negro woman had waited upon him and served him without recompense. She had no freedom of choice, no more personal rights than an iron kettle hanging on the kitchen wall. Now she was to be sold—like a kettle.

He could find no resolution for his thoughts; he could make no decision; when at last he undressed and slid into bed he fell asleep under a heavy burden of doubt.

He walked reluctantly to the shop next morning, knowing that his employer would appear shortly after, bringing the slave to be sold, her scanty possessions tied in a bundle. As he unlocked the shop door he realized that he was resigning himself to the situation. He was employed by the year to do his master's bidding and transact his master's business affairs; so he would have to draw up the loathsome bill of sale.

He felt a little eased in his mind when a member of his own Society appeared at the shop and anounced that he was the purchaser. At least, the Negro woman would not be falling into unkind hands.

6

THE MINISTRY

He wanted to talk it over with Elizabeth. The sister, who had
been his religious intimate for so long before she left home to
take up her residence and trade in Haddonfield, was a companion whom John Woolman sought out whenever he could
make the journey. Mounted on a good horse and traveling
alone, he could reach Haddonfield in less than a day. The road
from Mount Holly to Haddonfield took a more southerly
direction than the one to Cooper's Ferry and Philadelphia.
On the way he would cross a south branch of the Rancocas
River, ride past Darnell's Mills and Evesboro, coming out at
last on the village of Haddonfield.

He arrived at Elizabeth's house late in the afternoon to find
her preparing to pay a visit to Elizabeth Haddon Estaugh.
Why not go with her? He was friendly with the Estaughs, too.
He and Elizabeth could talk as they rode.

Quakers visiting Haddonfield automatically visited at the home of John and Elizabeth Estaugh. Haddon Hall, with its English box hedge and yew trees, its great rooms, its brew house and farm buildings, entertained many names that are prominent in Quaker history.

Elizabeth Haddon had built the home so famous for its hospitality in a clearing in the wilderness, and around it had grown up the village of Haddonfield. Her interest in the wild and far-off America had begun when she was only five, while she was still in England. William Penn had paid her family in London a visit, telling her father tales of the New World, of religious liberty, of the Indians and their customs, of wigwams, canoes, and wampum. He made the little Quaker girl a present of a mocassin. The memory of the mocassin never died, and when Elizabeth was eleven a Quaker preacher named John Estaugh visited London Yearly Meeting, and her father entertained him overnight. John Estaugh had just come from America. He brought ears of Indian corn, a food strange to many Europeans. By the time Elizabeth Haddon was eighteen she had quite made up her mind to see America, and she persuaded her father to let her occupy some lands he had acquired there. Accompanied by other migrating Friends, she left England and settled in West New Jersey, where she eventually married the same John Estaugh.

When Elizabeth and John Woolman rode up to the door, dismounted, and entered the warm living room with its huge fireplace ornamented with imported tiles, its cupboards with glass doors, its mahogany furniture and fine china, they were already friends of John and Elizabeth Estaugh of long standing. Elizabeth Haddon Estaugh by then was a woman of sixty-odd years who had been clerk of the women's Monthly Meeting of Haddonfield for thirty-seven years. She and her husband were famous among both Indians and settlers for their knowledge of medicine and nursing, their constant devotion to the sick and needy.

The two Elizabeths clasped hands. Now that Elizabeth Woolman was a tailor she often sewed for the residents of Haddon Hall.

Why not stay the night and attend First Day Meeting at Haddonfield tomorrow? they were asked.

The Woolmans needed little urging.

John Woolman's father was glad to know of his son's new resolution about slavery when John returned to the farmhouse on the Rancocas for a visit.

"I agree with thee, John," said Samuel. "And I am happy for thee."

John Woolman could hardly keep up with the growth of his own courage as he strode along the Jersey roadways and trails, consulting first this Friend, then that, on the question of slavery.

The issue wasn't new, at least not to Friends. The first official Friends' protest against slavery had been voiced in Germantown Meeting in 1688, and the Meeting passed the concern on to Yearly Meeting in Philadelphia. Not until eight years later did Yearly Meeting adopt a minute against the "bringing in of any more Negroes," but the agitation grew slowly, affecting the thinking of more and more members. Woolman had just reached his own point of decision, and so the issue was new to him because it was so newly illumined.

First Day Meetings for Worship in both Mount Holly and Rancocas began to hear the inspired voice of John Woolman speaking to their Christian consciences, and at Monthly Meeting Uncle Joseph Burr could sit with a little constraint in his manner and a little discomfort in his heart as he heard his nephew speak to the issue of the slaves which he himself owned.

Peter Andrews and his brother Isaac always responded to Woolman's warm, infectious enthusiasms; and at the next Yearly Meeting—at nearby Burlington in 1742—Anthony Benezet listened intently while Woolman told him about his ideas on slavery.

"It is against all Christian doctrine," said Woolman, and Anthony Benezet nodded in agreement.

"Further, I think," Benezet began, "that they are as gifted and intelligent as we. Could they be educated, they would accomplish much, I feel sure."

Schooling for Negroes was just the seedling of a dream in Benezet's mind then, a dream that still has not achieved its full growth.

"They have suffered much, captured from their own land and impressed into perpetual service," Woolman went on.

The two young men stimulated each other's thinking to the point of excitement. They walked on together, talking rapidly, as their conversation leaped from one subject to another.

"Art thou still working for the printer in Germantown?" Woolman asked.

"No," Benezet explained, and he seemed eager to tell of a new good fortune. "I have just begun to teach at the William Penn Charter School in Philadelphia."

He was using only gentleness on his pupils, he assured Woolman, as he guided them through the difficulties of writing, ciphering, accounting, and French (his native tongue). There was to be none of that acceptable teaching device of the times, the caning of bare backs.

Through the several days of the annual conference John Woolman discussed his concern with as many as he could meet; and he was deeply gratified and encouraged when the

Yearly Meeting, to which his own father was a Quarterly Meeting representative, included in its records the following minute:

"This Meeting repeats the caution against Friends importing Negroes and buying them after they are imported."

The minute could not be absolute—not yet—because Friends were not all of a single mind on the question of slavery, and only when there was unanimity of opinion would they be able to take a final stand. Too many prosperous Friends owned slaves and depended upon slave services to allow their consciences complete latitude in the matter. Slavery was part of the pattern of the times; it could not be changed overnight, nor over many nights.

John Woolman treasured the memory of that meeting when he was back in Mount Holly. There was hope; there could be a way eventually—if he kept his faith. Friends who had gathered in Burlington had had other concerns more pressing than his—the Indians, for instance—but they had taken the time to consider slavery, too.

The danger of disrupted friendship with the Indians was much more apparent than any dangers that could arise out of treating a few slaves considerately. Only the previous summer the government of Pennsylvania had held a big conference in Philadelphia with the Six Nations, the Iroquois Indians who lived chiefly in New York State. The conference had been held to persuade the Iroquois to remain on the side of the English in the colonial war that was going on and not to side with the French. For if such a great horde of Indians should change their allegiance, the English colonies of New York, Pennsylvania, and others would be in grave danger, since the Iroquois were powerful and had tremendous influence with other tribes. They even claimed jurisdiction over the Delawares.

The Meeting for Worship was always the Friends' primary and fundamental source of strength and direction. To it John Woolman turned with constancy and devotion, sometimes sitting in deep silence, sometimes rising to speak out; growing, growing, growing in his own personality and spiritual strength.

He did not go unnoticed. When young men like John Woolman showed such genuine interest in their faith and such real talent for conveying the Friendly message, the Society must needs make the most of their gifts.

Friends believe that every member of the Meeting for Worship is in reality a minister, and they do not have a separate ministry or priesthood especially trained, ordained, and paid a salary to lead the congregation. They believe that every worshiper is individually responsible for the success of the meeting. But in every group there are always a few who are outstanding, more concerned and more eloquent than others and especially able to contribute to the depths of worship. Those individuals are often designated as ministers and elders and given more responsibility than others.

The elders were watching John Woolman.

Eleven months passed, with their fall and winter and spring, and John joined his family to travel to the Monthly Meeting at Burlington. His thoughts were really on the next Yearly Meeting coming up, when he would see Anthony Benezet once more. His heart was grieved and sorely tried by the slowness with which Friends reached decisions, but he also knew that once they had arrived at a decision they would move heaven and earth to execute it. Friends could never be driven or forced; they could only be persuaded, stimulated, led. He experienced a little fleeting feeling of boyish foolishness when he caught himself dreaming of doing that persuading and leading.

"I must not think vain thoughts," he chided himself.

As he walked about the grounds of the Burlington Meeting House, he tried to imagine a world in which no slavery existed. It was a far-fetched dream.

He heard hurrying footsteps and a young woman's voice, "Please wait, John Woolman. I want to talk to thee."

It was Sarah Ellis, his cousin-by-marriage, who had been living with the Burrs for nearly four years. She was out of breath and excited.

"I have news for thee!" she gasped, and forgot decorum so far as to take hold of his hand.

Her touch sent a little tingle up his arm, and he made a special effort not to let it show in his manner.

"I hope I am the first to tell thee," she went on.

"I have heard nothing."

"It is about Uncle Joseph. He is considering freeing his slaves."

John Woolman completely forgot to be shy as he gazed into his cousin's eyes and found understanding there.

"It means," Sarah hurried to explain, even though she knew he would realize, "that if he frees them they will receive compensation for any work they do for us, and if they wish to leave us we will be unable to detain them once the papers have been drawn."

"They will not leave Peachfields," he assured her happily.

His own uncle had been reached by the message in John Woolman's heart! Surely God would grant him the power to speak to the condition of others.

Sarah had known how happy the news would make him, and she spoke gaily:

"Thou must return with us to Peachfields after Monthly Meeting. Now I must go."

He suddenly realized that he had been holding her hand in

both of his, and so tightly that the blood had quite left her fingers.

Sarah disappeared from sight, and he entered the men's meeting and sat down next to his father in such an excitement of mind that it required most of the period of silence to discipline himself to calmness.

"I shall not speak on any subject until I am completely myself," he resolved.

Respectfully he watched as the clerk stood up and declared the Meeting for Worship completed and the business meeting begun and the assistant clerk prepared to record the proceedings. The clerk's task was multifold. He had to guide the discussions, listen to expressions of concern, and take the sense of the meeting on every issue. His task was to know, through his own experience in Friends' matters and his own sensitivity, when, and if, there was unanimity of opinion, because votes were never taken.

The clerk asked for the report of the Meeting of Ministers and Elders, and a weighty Friend stood up and turned to face the gathering.

"After much searching of our minds we wish to recommend to the meeting that Peter Andrews, John Woolman, and Josiah White be designated as ministers."

John Woolman sat suddenly rigid, his pulse racing, not daring even to turn and look at his father, who must have known this was going to happen, since he himself was a minister and must have participated in that searching of minds. And Peter Andrews, too!

A short pause followed the announcement, and then, one after another, several Friends stood and approved the recommendation with words of commendation for the three young men. At a time such as this the clerk had no difficulty in taking the sense of the meeting, and the final minute inscribed in longhand in the minute book read:

"First day of Sixth Month, 1743— Whereas our friends Peter Andrews, John Woolman, and Josiah White have had at times a concern on their minds to appear in public by way of exhortation to religious duties, whose appearances are generally well received; wherefore a motion was made here that they might be recommended to sit in the Meeting of Ministers and Elders and they are hereby accordingly recommended."

When the business meeting was at last concluded, John Woolman rose in place and clasped hands with his father, then bounced away to find Peter Andrews. The two young men walked out into the warm summer air, excited, eager to find themselves some mission appropriate to their new responsibility. Perhaps they would be able to travel around and visit other meetings in New Jersey; intervisitation, especially by designated ministers, was a Friendly custom.

John Woolman's opportunity came shortly after, but much to his disappointment he and Peter Andrews were not to travel together. It did not occur to the Meeting to send out two untried, inexperienced young men. Instead, Abraham Farrington, nearly thirty years older than Woolman, well-seasoned in the affairs of the church, invited John Woolman to bear him company on a trip to the eastern parts of New Jersey.

This was to be John Woolman's first religious journey.

7

SLAVERY NORTH AND SOUTH

The two men set out on horseback, their leather breeches and jackets, hand-knit socks, and heavy shoes protecting them against the frost-laden November air. The route took them almost due north at first and then bore to the east. They traveled over one of New Jersey's oldest roads, which, like many others, had begun as an Indian trail through the forest.

The wilderness was disappearing from New Jersey, and the closer Woolman and Farrington came to New Brunswick, the Raritan River valley, and the Atlantic coast, the oftener they saw farmhouses surrounded by cultivated fields and fruit orchards. At last they reached New Brunswick, on the south bank of the Raritan, center of the prosperous agricultural area, with its brick houses and mills that took advantage of the water power.

To Abraham Farrington it was entirely familiar, but to John

Woolman it was all new, the world outside, land to see and explore. He was really a traveling Quaker at last, a carrier of the message to new places.

"Had an evening meeting at a tavern in Brunswick, a town in which none of our Society dwelt; the room was full and the people quiet."

The next morning the travelers pushed on, across the Raritan River by ferry, through the now hilly countryside to the seacoast and Perth Amboy.

All through the journey so far, John Woolman had tried to be considerate of his companion, tried not to plague him with too many foolish questions, had made every effort to be calm and dignified—and silent. But when they reached the prosperous seaport town and walked through its streets, Woolman began to see the real roots of the evil he abhorred most and to experience a deep shock. Shiploads of freshly captured human cargo were brought into Perth Amboy, dragged up out of the stinking holds of ships, and kept in huge stowage barracks until they could be sold at public auction. At least part of Perth Amboy's prosperity was due to the fact that it was a slave-trading center.

Woolman and Farrington wasted no time. They held a meeting that same evening at the courthouse and were pleased to see the room fill up and even to note the arrival of some members of the Assembly. A good portion of Perth Amboy's population was Quaker at that time, but it was apparent from the crowd that many more than Quakers had come.

Abraham Farrington, the seasoned and experienced minister, spoke eloquently and moved the meeting with his message, but Woolman was too troubled and disturbed by what he was seeing on the coast to be able to speak in that meeting or in others they held.

On this trip, for the first time in his life Woolman was really seeing the world that existed outside of his Quaker community. There were plenty of non-Friends in Philadelphia, to be sure, but he had never really come into contact with them. He had traveled in his own circle. The outside world must be vast if this was a sample! And the world's people . . . well . . . they were wicked. There was a little note of satisfaction, though, in the respect that the world's people felt for Friends. In the eyes of the outside world the Friends were persons of integrity, to be trusted and respected and consulted.

Farrington was assuming the responsibility of preaching at meeting after meeting on this, John Woolman's first religious journey. Woolman's silence broke its bounds when they finally left Perth Amboy and pushed on to Rahway and Plainfield. He talked volubly and long about the evils of slavery, and the older man let the younger work off his shock.

There was a war consciousness along the coast that had startled Woolman, too, who had never before realized how protected Philadelphia was, so far up the Delaware River. Perth Amboy wasn't far from New York, another international port, where ships of war might come and go, or even attack. The conflict between England and Spain (and, before much longer, France) was much more threatening to residents along the coast. And Perth Amboy was on the mail route. The postman rode down from Boston to New York and on through Perth Amboy, bringing letters and newspapers full of news from abroad.

Woolman gradually recovered his equilibrium as he and Farrington visited twelve more meetings in nearby towns, and at last they turned their horses' heads southward once more and returned home. They had been away two weeks.

Woolman left Abraham Farrington at his home in Burlington and went on to Mount Holly. There was exactly one thing that he wanted to do: to talk about all that he had experienced on his journey. He wanted particularly to talk with Peter Andrews—and with Sarah Ellis.

This visit to Peachfields was not his first. The big fieldstone house that stood in the midst of fifteen hundred acres of peach orchards saw Cousin John oftener and oftener as his interest in Sarah Ellis deepened. When he galloped his horse up to the house once more, the Burrs hurried to let him in, because they all wanted to hear about his mission to East Jersey. News brought home by traveling Friends was always welcome.

"Good day, Cousin John," said one after another.

There were Uncle Joseph and Aunt Jane, Cousin Henry, who now owned the nearby farmland, and Cousin Joseph, who owned a sawmill in Mount Holly—and Sarah Ellis. John Woolman glanced at the brown-skinned faces in the household and felt redeemed and restored. These slaves could expect to be freed.

The huge fireplace with its crackling logs and warmth was the largest in all of Burlington County. John Woolman walked toward it as soon as he had shed his outside jacket and let its glow drive away the chill of the November day. He turned around to see Sarah Ellis smiling at him.

"We've waited for thee to return and tell us of thy journey," she said. "Wilt thou take supper with us?"

It was still early in the afternoon, but Woolman was glad for the invitation, because he wanted to stay a long time. The rest of the family had left them alone, and John and Sarah took chairs close to the hearth.

He began to relate to her the discoveries of his journey to East New Jersey: New Brunswick, Perth Amboy. And the seacoast—he had never seen it before. Since she had lived near Shrewsbury, it must not be news to her, but . . .

She nodded her interest. "It is like a return journey," she assured him.

He told her about the profound impression that had been made by Abraham Farrington's preaching. John Woolman talked on, because he liked to talk, and because Sarah Ellis liked to listen to him, and because she liked to watch his sensitive face so full of the animation and ardor and purpose he felt.

When the subject of the journey was spent, there was much more to discuss: his work, for instance.

"Dost thou like tailoring?" Sarah prompted him.

John Woolman had recently determined to learn the craft, because he knew he must settle on some kind of trade for himself.

"It seems to be a good way to earn a living—*in case I should settle*," he hinted timidly to Sarah. "My master was once a tailor, and he has taught me a great deal. I have already done some work for Elizabeth Estaugh. I can work on it whenever business in the shop is slack . . . and . . . a handicraft frees my mind for meditation."

They sat in silence for a few moments, until Sarah looked toward the window. A quiet, gentle snowfall had begun. They got up and walked toward the window to watch through the imperfectly made window glass with its tiny bubbles and iridescent ripples.

"Snow is pretty," said Sarah, "but I wish it were summer so that we could walk out."

"I wish," said John Woolman, taking hold of her hand, "that it were spring, and that all the peach trees were in blossom."

They were unaware that a chill had crept into the room, until Uncle Joseph came in and said:

"What has become of the fire?"

Startled, the young people looked toward the fireplace. The fire had died down while they had sat right in front of it and watched it disappear. Joseph Burr said no more, but with a vague smile on his lips he picked up the fire irons and started to retrieve the hot embers that remained. John Woolman leaped forward to help his uncle lift a fresh log into place.

All through the rest of the winter, John Woolman worked at his tailoring trade, finding the hand of Providence in it, because:

"I saw the happiness of humility and laboured for it, and in this labour I was often in supplication to the Most High and in some of these private exercises my mind was so environed with Heavenly Light and consolation that it made things easy which had been otherways."

Patience was the virtue he needed to strive for most, because he was still too young to deserve the full confidence of the Meeting elders. They doled responsibilities slowly, appointing him to short-lived committees for this purpose and that, listening with increasing satisfaction to his messages in Meeting for Worship; but another opportunity to travel abroad as a minister did not come right away.

He sat with Peter Andrews in Monthly Meetings and Quarterly Meetings and yearned to be older and steadier and more trusted. He sat in Yearly Meeting (this time in Burlington) with Peter Andrews and Anthony Benezet, and here his responsibilities were progressively less in the face of so many weighty members drawn from so much wider an area.

Aware of his own vanity, John Woolman closed his eyes for a moment to realign his attitude. Of course, others had more responsibility than he! They were older, more seasoned, more capable. He must wait upon the Lord for guidance and direction. He must wait—with infinite patience—through all of his life if need be.

A rustle and stir and metallic clank caused him to open his

eyes, and he suddenly saw all of Quaker orthodoxy about to be threatened by an insane and outlandish prank.

It was Benjamin Lay again!

The uncouth, misshapen fellow had dressed himself in a plain greatcoat fastened with one button. Down the aisle he marched, completely disregarding the jurisdiction of the clerks, and turned and faced the assemblage.

"Oh, all you Negro masters," he rasped, "who are contentedly holding your fellow creatures in a state of slavery during life, well knowing the cruel sufferings those innocent captives undergo in their state of bondage, both in these North American colonies, and in the West India islands; you must know they are not made slaves by any direct law, but are held by an arbitrary and self-interested custom in which you participate."

When Lay paused for breath, there was not even the stirring of a particle of dust in the room. They had not *wanted* to discuss slavery again; yet every year someone persisted in raising the question. There was too much divergence of opinion to reach a conclusion. Lay must realize that.

"And *especially you who profess to do unto all men as ye would they should do unto you*," the little eccentric persisted, "and yet, in direct opposition to every principle of reason, humanity, and religion, you are forcibly retaining your fellow men, from one generation to another, in a state of unconditional servitude; you might as well throw off the plain coat as I do. . . ."

With a wide sweep of his arm he threw aside his topcoat and stood before them dressed in a military uniform, a sword buckled to his side, a large book under his arm.

"It would be as justifiable in the sight of the Almighty," he went on, "who beholds and respects all nations and colours of men with an equal regard, if you should thrust a sword through their hearts as I do through this book."

Beside himself with excitement, Benjamin Lay whipped the sword from its sheath and stabbed the book. But it was not just a book. Its pages had been removed and he had concealed an animal's bladder full of red pokeberry juice inside it. The sharp sword penetrated the bladder and sent the "blood" squirting and splattering all over the Friends sitting within Lay's range.

Shocking scene! Even if Lay was right, he had used a most intemperate and unseemly approach to the issue.

John Woolman experienced a sharp grief, the kind that comes from sudden tragedy; he was mute, yet bursting to speak; wordless, at this time when inspired leadership could have recovered the Yearly Meeting from its experience. Was there none present to rise? Apparently not.

As soon as the Meeting adjourned, he and Benezet walked outside and began to converse in low tones.

"If only he had not done such a thing . . ."

"Yet he is right," said Woolman.

"Yes, but he cannot convert Friends in such a manner."

"No."

"He did another frightful thing recently," said Benezet. "He stole a neighbor's child and hid him all day. When the frantic parents finally came upon him and told him their story, he said, 'Your child is safe in my house, and you may now conceive of the sorrow you inflicted upon the parents of the Negro girl you hold in slavery, for she was torn from them by avarice.' "

"One cruelty cannot cure another!" Woolman almost cried.

"How can we speak to Friends' hearts about slavery?" asked Anthony Benezet, addressing his words partly to himself and partly to Woolman.

"The truth must reach every single heart," said Woolman.

"When that is accomplished, Friends will be united on the question."

Every single heart was the thought Woolman took back to Mount Holly with him and turned over and over in his mind as he sewed. A coat was not made all at once, but by every single stitch, one following another in reasonable order, until at last, seams matched, sleeves set in place, edges turned, the whole garment emerged.

He began to consult tactfully with one neighbor and another, day after day, gently testing their feelings on slavery, finding favorable responses in more Friends than actually had the courage to act. The end of slavery was far off, but it was somewhere, Woolman firmly believed.

He was irked by the amount of time he had to give to earning a living, when he would rather have been abroad preaching gospel. A man ought not to think any more than absolutely necessary about the earning of creaturely goods, and he ought to keep his needs to a minimum so that his spirit will be as free as possible of worldliness.

When his employer said that he intended to give up his shop altogether, John Woolman welcomed the opportunity to become self employed. Perhaps he ought to buy this shop or some shop of his own. Yet that would tie him down again. Shop-keeping required a great deal of attention and effort. He really need not make the decision in a hurry; he had been frugal and had saved his money.

So, for a while, John Woolman's only lucrative activity was his tailoring, and as he stitched he thought. His thoughts began to marshal themselves into a single idea: a journey into the Southland to investigate slavery there.

"I feel a deep exercise to travel southward," he confided in Peter Andrews.

"So does Isaac," Peter told him. "Thou must go to Haddon-field and talk to him."

Woolman would rather have traveled with Peter, but he knew his friend could not take two or three months away from his work. He discovered that Peter's brother shared his concern, and the two men applied to their Monthly Meeting for permission to go forth on their proposed religious mission. Permission was granted, and they were given the necessary certificates, or letters of introduction, to be presented to any meetings they might visit on their journey.

On the twelfth day of the third month (May) in the year 1746, John Woolman and Isaac Andrews started out, covering the familiar route to Cooper's Ferry, crossing the Delaware River at Philadelphia, and turning southward into Chester County, Pennsylvania.

Woolman still felt a little piqued within himself about having to travel with Isaac instead of Peter. He could get on with almost anyone, and he and Isaac were really friends; but it would have been so much easier with Peter; Peter was like another facet of himself.

He and Isaac crossed the Susquehanna River and came upon a region known as the Red Lands, where the "poorer sort of people" were trying to survive the hardships of the wilderness. Their houses were primitive, their manners and talk uncouth, and Woolman had to remind himself to examine into the spirit and ignore the surface symptoms, because these "poorer people" welcomed the visiting ministers and shared with them what they had as well as they knew how. The worst hardships of the wilderness had all been overcome in Rancocas and Mount Holly by the time John Woolman entered the world, and this glimpse of the Red Lands was a leavening glimpse of the past.

He and Isaac and a guide rode on south across the western

shore—western side of Chesapeake Bay—of Maryland to Fairfax County, Virginia, where they held meetings at Manoquacy, Fairfax, Hopewell, and Shenando.

How worldly the world, and how creaturely its creatures! Very different motives had gone into the founding of Virginia than of Pennsylvania. Virginia's early settlers had come for profit, pure and simple, and they had soon discovered that their profit could be found in the wicked weed called tobacco. At first they grew it by their own efforts on small farms. But in 1619 the first slave ship to touch the mainland of what is now the United States put in at Jamestown and sold the Virginia planters "twenty Negers." This new kind of cheap hand labor was ideal for tobacco growing, and soon the small farms vanished in the wake of huge plantations.

To the two modestly homespun visitors on horseback who came to talk of equality, humility, and self-restraint, the tragic extremes of wealth and human misery were a shocking awakening. They had read about and heard about these conditions, but they had not before experienced them, had not realized how awful they really were. There could be no doubt in either of their minds that the fruits of human bondage could be only evil.

As they pushed southward through Virginia to Perquimans in North Carolina, no longer using a guide, conditions grew no better. Sometimes they slept in the forest; sometimes they were the embarrassed guests in wealthy homes, knowing that their comforts grew out of the wretchedness of the Negro cabins.

Yet the zealous young missionaries could not help but realize that wherever they went some hearts opened to them. In North Carolina Woolman was profoundly aware of the interest of young people in his message. The situation in the Southland, however shocking, was full of hope.

George Fox had visited Virginia, Maryland, and Carolina

on his trip to America scarcely seventy-five years earlier, and he had left the stamp of his personality there forever. Friends had settled in these areas before Fox's visit. He convinced many more, and their numbers continued to increase. Woolman and Andrews had found a Monthly Meeting in Hopewell that was ten years old and a brand new Monthly Meeting in Fairfax.

"There is much to hope for here," he said to Isaac Andrews in an earnest tone of voice, and Isaac Andrews agreed.

After their visits in North Carolina they turned northward again into Virginia, and when they reached the James River they followed its bank upstream to the mountains, where there was a new settlement. The lonely, isolated settlers were overjoyed to see them. Whenever the young men found "honest hearted friends who appeared to be concerned for the cause of truth" they rejoiced.

"From Virginia we crossed over the river Potomac at Hoe's Ferry, and made a general visit to the Meetings of Friends on the western shore of Maryland, were also at their Quarterly Meeting at Herring Creek. . . ."

They journeyed homeward, and on the way back Woolman rode deep in thought much of the time. Two things in particular bothered him. He had accepted hospitality free of cost from people who lived lives of ease and drew their comforts from the toil of slaves. The other was the slave trade itself and its terrific hold on the social life of the South.

"I saw so many vices and corruptions spreading, in a great measure occasioned by this trade and way of life, that it appeared to me as a dark gloominess hanging over the land; and though now many do willingly run into it, yet in future the consequences will be grievous to posterity. I express it as it appeared to me not once nor twice but as a matter fixed in my mind."

8

A MATTER FIXED IN HIS MIND

John Woolman was so filled with his concern about slavery after his trip through the South that he could think and speak of nothing else. He expressed it many times, a matter fixed in his mind, to every Friend willing to listen. Some he found who would wholeheartedly say, "I agree with thee," or "I plan to free my slaves," or "I have long since given up my slaves." He found others who agreed with him but admitted they could not face the thought of having to do without the services of their own slaves, and more who simply turned tight-lipped and silent when the subject was broached.

There was no doubt, however, in the mind of any last remaining elder as to John Woolman's capacity for the ministry, and his Quarterly Meeting designated him a representative to Yearly Meeting directly upon his return from the South. John Woolman responded with gratitude and humility; so great had his mission grown that it had supplanted youthful vanity.

Immediately after Yearly Meeting, even though the fall weather was far advanced, he and Peter Andrews made a journey of almost a month's duration to the Jersey seacoast, visiting Friends and their Meetings in Salem, Cape May, Great and Little Egg Harbor.

"By computation three hundred and forty miles," John Woolman recorded. He did not set down in his journal how happy he was to be traveling with Peter.

They worked their way up the miles and miles of flat, uninhabited sandy coast to present their credentials at last at Meetings in Barnegat, Manahockin, and Squan, and from there they were fortunate enough to arrive in time for the Yearly Meeting at Shrewsbury. Abraham Farrington was visiting Shrewsbury, too, and the companion of John Woolman's first journey clasped his hand warmly and asked after his progress.

Winter weather was well upon them when he and Peter Andrews returned to Mount Holly, but nevertheless John Woolman made his calls to those who would want detailed news of his trip: his parents and family in Rancocas, the Burrs and Sarah Ellis at Peachfields, and his sister Elizabeth in Haddonfield.

Elizabeth was still his closest confidante, and while he was free of fixed employment he called at her home again and again. He could sit quietly near her as she sewed, sometimes talking, sometimes silent.

Later that winter, on one of these visits, he told her that he had committed some of his thoughts about slavery to paper. He took out the pages.

"Read it to me," she encouraged him, and he began to read parts of his now renowned essay, "Some Considerations on the Keeping of Negroes."

"It would be the highest wisdom to forego customs and

popular opinions, and try the treasures of the soul by the infallible standard TRUTH," said the opening sentence of his introduction.

Elizabeth nodded. She, more than anyone else, knew how many careful hours since his southern journey, how much meditation, must have gone into the writing of this essay. Truth! That was what her brother sought. That was his real dedication, the real goal of his life, his prayers, and his journeyings. It was the falsehood in slaveholding that disturbed him, the falsehood in betraying the Indians with rum, the falsehood in praying to a God of peace and then supporting a war.

She listened with head bowed over her sewing as he read through the introduction and began the main body of the essay:

"There are various circumstances amongst them that keep Negroes, and different ways by which they fall under their care; and, I doubt not, there are many well-disposed persons amongst them, who desire rather to manage wisely and justly in this difficult matter, than to make gain of it," he read on, and from one page to the next he gradually developed his understanding of true Christian doctrine.

"To consider mankind otherwise than brethren, to think favours are peculiar to one nation, and exclude others, plainly supposes a darkness in the understanding. For, as God's love is universal, so where the mind is sufficiently influenced by it, it begets a likeness of itself, and the heart is enlarged towards all men."

He built point upon point in his exquisite prose, documenting each with references from his beloved Scriptures.

It was a long essay. There were several pages more. When at last he read the closing sentences and looked up, he discovered that his sister was weeping.

"Thou wilt show the essay to Father," whispered Elizabeth.

When he took his departure that day, John Woolman held his horse to a walk and rode with lowered head, grateful for the sympathetic persons with whom his life was filled. He and they were free to follow their peculiar purist patterns without interference in this little world that William Penn had created. No whippings, floggings, or foul imprisonments here as there had been in England and even in New England. Peter and Isaac Andrews' own grandmother had been stripped to the waist as a young woman, tied to the rear end of a cart by an angry Boston mob, and whipped out of town for daring to invade that Puritan stronghold with Quaker doctrine.

He returned to Haddonfield a few days later for another talk with Elizabeth and noted that his sister lacked animation.

"I feel a sadness that I cannot explain," she told him. "I feel dejected and disconsolate."

"Thou hast no grief with anyone?"

She shook her head. Perhaps it would pass. Perhaps she had been attempting too much work.

After the passing of another couple of days John Woolman was summoned to her bedside. Elizabeth Haddon Estaugh, angel of all the sick, was already there, and so was John's mother, to tell him that his sister had contracted smallpox.

Smallpox was a scourge of the century. Few escaped it; many died of it; all lived in terror of it. Sometimes an epidemic swept through a community, and sometimes it appeared in a few individual cases.

Elizabeth's feelings of sadness and dejection had been the evil disease incubating in her system, until all of a sudden her temperature rose, her pulse began to race, her head ached, and no food would stay on her stomach. Automatically her neighbors came to her side. After another three days the red ugly rash that could be measles or scarlet fever began to appear, and when the red lumps began to show at the roots of her hair her family and friends were sure of the worst: the terrible disfiguring smallpox. Even if Elizabeth lived through it, she would never be attractive-looking again but would wear forever on her face the pits and scarrings of the running sores that were going to develop.

Even though smallpox was infamous for the ease with which it could travel from one person to another, Elizabeth Woolman never lacked for nursing care and comforting companions as she lay in bed. The red lumps began to break out all over her body as her mother and Elizabeth Estaugh did all they knew how. The village doctor came with his scanty knowledge.

The red lumps enlarged and filled with fluid; the skin around each became inflamed and swollen.

John sat by her side every day, reading to her or listening closely when there was something on her heart that she wanted to speak about. The brother and sister were drawn closer together, and for the first time Elizabeth began to tell John about her own youth.

"When I was a girl, I was wanton and airy, but I thought I had thoroughly repented for it."

Elizabeth's throat and mouth were too sore for her to speak above a whisper, and her vision was fading.

It was small wonder that she had been able to understand her brother's spiritual struggles and conflicts, his vacillating back and forth between the tavern and the meetings. She had lived through them herself in an earlier year. Perhaps her decision to leave her family and live in a house of her own with only a servant for company had had something to do with her longing for a more religious life. She had chosen a handicraft to earn her living, just as he had done, so that her mind would be free for contemplation.

Her affliction progressed from day to day, the fever temporarily receding while the eruptions matured. When the sores had lived their life, they would form scabs and the itch would drive the patient into delirium.

Elizabeth's hope had not yet flagged. This was the kind of divine discipline through which one must often suffer.

Because she had ministered to so many others in their sicknesses, friends and neighbors came from miles around to bring her necessary gifts and encouragement. But Elizabeth knew the progress of the disease as well as any of them, and by the middle of the second week, when her temperature began to climb again, her hope disappeared.

"The Lord hath rewarded me sevenfold, and I am unable to express the greatness of his love manifested to me."

When she saw her mother weeping, it was the stricken woman who comforted the well: "Dear Mother, weep not for me; I go to my God."

The Woolmans and their neighbors hoped against hope that the rising fever was causing delirium, that it would pass somehow and that Elizabeth would be spared. But when another neighbor entered, late to the situation, Elizabeth spoke clearly, "I have had a hard night, but shall not have another such, for I shall die, and it will be well with my soul."

Elizabeth sank into a coma that same day and by nightfall she was dead. Like the flickering candlelight that illuminated her bedroom, her life grew weaker and more uncertain until it disappeared.

Quaker training shows its greatest strength under its severest trials. With heroic self-restraint the grief-stricken Woolmans set about making final arrangements for the interment of this daughter who had been taken from them in her thirty-first year. There would be no costly funeral, no vain displays. Elizabeth Woolman would be laid modestly to rest in the Friends' graveyard. The stone which marked her grave would bear no eulogies, and some Friends of the times even felt that the mere stone itself was a vanity.

To John Woolman fell the responsibility of settling his sister's estate, and he moved about with wooden precision, making an inventory of her effects, looking through the papers. He sat at her writing table and for a few brief moments let grief sweep over him. This understanding companion, this woman who had been a second mother, this constant source of strength. . . .

He began to read her will. To her father she had left her great Bible, to her mother her looking glass, to John the sum of twelve pounds and some gold buttons. There was money for Asher, Abner, Uriah, Jonah, Abraham, and Eber, and even sums for sisters Sarah, Hannah, Esther, and Rachel. Her household effects went to Hannah, and Patience received her best gowns.

Elizabeth, too, had committed some of her deepest thoughts to paper, John found.

"Oh, that my head were as waters and mine eyes as a fountain of tears, that I might weep day and night until acquainted with my God," he read.

His own eyes filled, and he laid the papers down with fumbling hands and went outside.

Peter Andrews, who knew John so well and was so sensitive to his moods, realized that this was a time when the minister needed a minister. He stayed with him as much as possible, offered gentle suggestions when he felt they were acceptable, and gradually persuaded John Woolman to think of resolving his own affairs as soon as his sister's were completed.

"Thou needest a home and a place of settlement like the rest of us."

Woolman did feel a little homeless now that Elizabeth was gone, but it did not occur to him to move farther away from

Rancocas than Mount Holly. A man did not deliberately cut himself off from those he loved and who supported him with their love. With Andrews encouraging him, he began to look about him for a means of support, and he finally purchased a brick house on 47 Mill Street in Mount Holly. It was a two-story affair with a door and two windows facing the street on the first floor, three windows on the second floor, and two dormer windows in the roof.

"I plan to open a shop," he explained.

It was a good idea, since he knew shopkeeping so well and could still ply his tailoring trade as well as write legal documents for his friends.

A month later he purchased a piece of farmland from Peter Andrews on Old Springfield Road (now Branch Street), a mere half mile out of town.

As soon as the transaction was completed, he and Peter Andrews began to talk about making a religious journey of serious length together, through Long Island and New England. Peter Andrews saw the real need that Woolman felt for a final healing salve to his sorrow, and so he left his own affairs in the hands of others and he and John Woolman obtained certificates from their Monthly Meeting. They expected to be gone all summer.

They set out across New Jersey and arrived in time for Yearly Meeting at Flushing, where there was a great assemblage of local Friends and Friends visiting from other parts of the colonies and from England. Woolman was obviously cheered by the time it was over.

He was still the young minister, rather dependent upon his older companion in spite of the compelling message he had to give on slavery; and at the outset of this trip he was a little constrained by his personal loss. A grief does not lose its edge hurriedly.

"We continued to visit the Meetings of Friends on this Island and through the mercies of the Almighty we were helped in the work."

Throughout the colonies, in the outlying areas where there was no Meeting House, one Friend or another would hold Meetings in his home; and those same homes served as oases of hospitality for traveling Friends. They visited such a Meeting at Oyster Bay, and then crossed over to the mainland to Meetings at Oblong and Nine Partners in New York.

"To love our children," he said to those who claimed they loved their slaves, "is needful; but except this love proceeds from the true heavenly principle which sees beyond earthly treasures, it will rather be injurious than of any real advantage to them: Where the fountain is corrupt, the streams must necessarily be impure."

He always had a message for the prosperous, particularly if they appeared too prosperous.

Woolman felt his old verve coming back when he watched the value of his teaching and preaching, especially among young people. He came upon a quantity of young members of the Society, "used often to spend their time together in merriment," and managed to reach them with his eloquence.

"As these stood steadfast to that inward convincement [which he had given them]," he wrote, "they were made a blessing to some of their former companions."

He and Peter Andrews went on through Connecticut, speaking sometimes to Friends, sometimes to groups of non-Friends, and after three days' hard riding they reached Rhode Island.

Rhode Island has been called the nursery of Quakerism in America. It was the first colony in the New World to guarantee religious liberty by law, and the earliest Friends' missionaries fled to Rhode Island seeking asylum from the persecutions in Massachusetts. Other Friends moved into Rhode Island and the Providence Plantations, others already living there were convinced by the Friends, and a Quaker community grew up many years before the founding of Pennsylvania.

On this trip through Rhode Island John Woolman struck up his friendship with Thomas Hazard. Thomas Hazard had become deeply exercised over the question of slavery when he was still a very young man. He took issue with his wealthy, slave-owning father at the risk of being disinherited, and farmed his own Narragansett acres with free labor. His action deeply affected the New England Meeting, and by 1744 it passed a minute "that Friends refrain from buying slaves when imported."

John Woolman arrived in 1747 to add his moral weight to that of Thomas Hazard's.

"The situation is still tragic," Woolman observed. "I see here huge land-owning planters operating with slave labor in a way that closely resembles the South."

He felt frustrated, inept, small, and weak in the face of such a mighty social force. Slavery was a growing, spreading, cancerous thing, and the numbers who were willing to fight it were woefully few.

Woolman's distress was dispelled somewhat by the prospect of seeing the city of Boston. Travel in its own right was adventuresome, and Woolman was still in his twenties.

But the first sight of Boston was a blow to the young man who had seen Philadelphia first. Boston was the biggest city in the English colonies, but that was its only claim to glory; it was crowded, unplanned, with narrow, crooked streets, and possessed none of the grace and charm of Philadelphia.

"Perhaps," Woolman suggested modestly to his companion as they approached the Meeting House on Congress Street (Quaker Lane), "we should be grateful that Friends are now allowed to convene in Massachusetts."

Peter shared his reaction, but Woolman's devoted friend was more concerned with watching Woolman show signs of being restored and refreshed by his journey. He was moving with his old vigor, and every Friend who was willing to listen to his message on slavery raised his morale another notch.

From Boston he and Peter returned to Newport and took a boat out to the lonely, isolated Island of Nantucket off the coast of Cape Cod.

The first white settlers had come to this treeless island with its moors and scrub oak and lichens a hundred years earlier, and by the beginning of the eighteenth century had turned to whaling to earn their livelihood. When Woolman paid Nantucket his first visit, he found that the islanders were skilled and daring seamen who owned a whole fleet of whaling vessels. He found, too, that a vast number of them were Quakers and very few of them slave owners.

He and Peter spent a whole week on Nantucket. When at last they crossed the Sound from New London to Long Island, John Woolman began to show a marked impatience to be home.

Peter Andrews knew he wanted to get his newly purchased shop into operation, and he smiled as he wondered what other secret motives John Woolman might have in mind.

9

A WELL-INCLINED DAMSEL

John Woolman plunged into the planning of his life with new zest. He worked hard to get his shop stocked and into operation, like a man who is anxious to finish this task because there is a more important one calling him. He must be ready by very early spring to tend the acres he had bought and set to rights the house that stood upon it. He had purchased orchard ground, and he intended to set in apple trees.

Life began to move at a new high rate of speed. Old enough by now to have mature dignity and still young enough to be blessed with an endless supply of driving energy, John Woolman was carving out the niche that he would occupy for the rest of his days.

All through the winter and summer of 1748 he developed and planned his farmland and tended his shop on Mill Street, walking the half mile back and forth between the two. In Oc-

tober he stopped from his labors long enough to go on a religious trip through the southern counties of New Jersey and
the eastern shore of Maryland with John Sykes, a member
of the Chesterfield Meeting. The journey through the inter-
vening stretches of wilderness, the visit at Friends' meetings,
the gentle pleading that he did with slaveholders, fed the
wellsprings of his spirit and quickened his concern for the enslaved blacks; and when he returned to Mount Holly after a
six weeks' absence he looked at his own land and reminded
himself that nothing would grow there except what had been
tended by his own and other free men's hands.

His lingering tendency to impatience still troubled him.
Farmland must await the seasons, and men's hearts must await
the Light; these things he knew, yet these things he could not
always remember. Even after so many years of successful striving and self-discipline, he found himself speaking with too
much heat at times, foolishly willing his trees to grow faster,
and walking the two miles to Peachfields with too much haste.

Sarah Ellis's patience was standing the test more stoically.
Hers was a gentle, devoted, self-effacing disposition, and if she
watched with anxious misgivings at the window for John
Woolman to come striding up to her uncle's house, she never
admitted it to this young man she was so deeply in love with.
When he extended an invitation to "come and visit at my
shop" or "come and see how the apple trees are budding,"
nothing detained her from accepting it.

After another spring had passed, John Woolman sought
out Sarah Ellis almost daily. He was ready at last; his life
was settled; he could presume to man's estate and take a wife.
But yesterday was the day his courage had failed and he had
not asked her; and today was another day when they strolled
along the curving roadway and he reasoned with himself that
he would see her again tomorrow and perhaps tomorrow he

would feel more determined. This was really proving as hard as the bill of sale decision.

Out of a long period of walking in silence together, he spoke to Sarah, "A man is often tested beyond his strength."

"I think thou couldst stand any test."

Quiet, gentle, and shy, Sarah was really braver than he, and he knew she read his mind.

"Maybe this summer, Sarah, or by the end of this summer . . ."

They stopped in the center of the road, in the glow of a late afternoon sun, and she looked up and liked the way his hair fell behind his ears without benefit of wig or ribbon or any adornment.

"By the end of this summer," he made a fresh start, "if thou wouldst . . . we could be wed."

"I have loved thee a long time, John Woolman."

That volatile strain in his disposition that would not be disciplined away betrayed his calm once more and he seized her hands.

"Then I shall kiss thee!"

Now hers was the panic and his the courage.

"In this roadway?" she gasped.

"There are none to see us but the wild birds and the grass-hoppers!"

"Well, perhaps if we walked through the orchard . . ."

"John Woolman and Sarah Ellis appeared before the Burlington Monthly Meeting on the fourth day of the seventh month (September), 1749 and declared their intentions of marriage with each other, it being the first time. The father of the young man being present expressed his consent and also said his wife consented. Josiah White and Thomas Busby are desired to make the necessary inquiry concerning the young couple and report to the next Meeting."

So says the record of the Monthly Meeting when the smiling and hopeful pair made their announcement to the surprise of none. They must wait a month, after the manner of Friends, because marriage was not a state to enter into carelessly or hastily. Consent of both families must be obtained by the committee, and the genuine intent and "freedom to wed" of both parties must be carefully examined. Sometimes the month's delay for consideration and examination of the circumstances resulted in denial of consent of the Meeting, but not in this instance, where everyone had known everyone else during all of their lives, and where both families were beginning to despair that the wedding would ever happen.

On the second day of the eighth month the committee reported back to the Monthly Meeting that it had found nothing to obstruct the intentions of the couple, and that left John and Sarah at liberty to accomplish their marriage "when they should see meete." They saw meete within a matter of days. Caleb Haines and Joseph Lippincott were then desired to attend the wedding and testify to its proper execution.

The summer had been spent in an excitement of fixing the house on Old Springfield Road, collecting gifts, putting finishing touches on dowry and wedding clothes. Now John and Sarah had suddenly to put aside their merriment and face the sobriety of their wedding day.

A Quaker wedding is a deeply moving and solemn affair, a very special Meeting for Worship, where the doctrine of simplicity and sincerity finds its purest expression.

They stood before the Mount Holly Meeting House, holding hands to give each other courage.

"I am truly quaking, John."

"I, too. It will be a long and trying affair."

"Other weddings seemed very beautiful. I always cry at weddings."

"Thou must not cry today."

"Oh, no! I feel very happy."

The bride's head was modestly covered with a small cap, and over her pale blue dress with its snug bodice she wore a covering apron of a dull green hue. (White was then considered gay and wanton.) The groom standing by her side wore a brand new, knee-length coat that he had fashioned with his own needle. His father had woven the woolen fabric, and it had been dyed blue at a Mount Holly dying mill. It was buttoned all the way down the front with the gold buttons that Elizabeth had bequeathed to him.

The Meeting was already assembled and waiting for them. They must go in. So, faces radiant, still holding hands, they stepped inside the door.

What had they feared or quaked about? These were all their own beloved group, friends and relatives, sitting in rows, eager for a glimpse of the bride and groom. On the facing seats were Samuel and Elizabeth Woolman, Uncle Joseph, and Aunt Jane.

John Woolman and Sarah Ellis walked down the aisle to the front and took their places on the facing seats.

None could preside at this sacred occasion save God Himself, and so all sat in silence for what may have been a quarter of an hour, until God could enter every heart. At long last the bride and groom rose in place, clasping hands, and faced that sea of watching eyes.

John Woolman made his declaration:

"In the presence of the Lord and before these Friends, I take thee, Sarah Ellis, to be my wife, promising, with divine assistance, to be unto thee a loving and faithful husband as long as we both shall live."

Sarah Ellis found her voice from somewhere and responded:

"In the presence of the Lord and before these Friends, I take thee, John Woolman, to be my husband, promising, with divine assistance, to be unto thee a loving and faithful wife as long as we both shall live."

That was all. No ring, no flowers, no attendants, no vows of obedience. The bride and groom sat down, and the Meeting re-entered its silent meditation. Messages of encouragement, blessing, and hopefulness gradually came from one member and another as the happy couple, now joined for life, held hands behind the privacy of the bride's wide skirts.

At the rise of the Meeting the newly married couple signed the contract spread upon a table, and many members came forward to sign it as witnesses.

There was plenty of joyous laughter and feasting after the serious part was done. The well-to-do Quaker farmers could set a sumptuous table throughout the year, and a wedding was an excellent time for housewives to vie with one another's skill.

John Woolman, in his twenty-ninth year, at long last led his bride to the home on Old Springfield Road, the one he had been preparing so long, surrounded by his newly planted orchards.

He was too shy to write about his courtship or his wedding, though, and he sums it all up in one precious sentence in his *Journal*:

"Believing it good for me to settle and thinking seriously about a companion, my heart was turned to the Lord with desires that He would give me wisdom to proceed therein agreeable to His will, and He was pleased to give me a well inclined damsel, Sarah Ellis, to whom I was married the 18th day of 8th month, 1749."

10

SOME CONSIDERATIONS ...

During the first year of his married life, John Woolman gave a great deal of his attention to getting his farm and shop into operation. In his shop he wanted to devote most of his energies to tailoring, but in response to the needs of his customers he began to stock "trimmings for garments, and from thence proceeded to sell cloths and linens." Before long he was selling "tea, thread, rum, molasses, butter, coffee, knitting needles, snuff, earthen dishes, chocolate, check, sheeting, tape, indigo, powder and shot, mettle buttons, silk, buckram, gloves, and cedar board."

His work and his joys and his concerns were now one. Sarah fitted into all of them with skill and sympathy and devotion. John Woolman's philosophy and faith were her own anyway, her training was identical with his, and it was only in his increasing excellence that she saw him move ahead of her and understood that while he served his God and his goals, her task in turn would be to serve him.

His religious purposes could flower in this new aura of understanding. He could commit more of the fruits of his meditations to paper, because Sarah created for him the opportunity for solitude as well as for companionship. Or he and she could think out loud together, and that, too, helped to resolve his thinking. Quakers believed in educating women equally with men, and Sarah Ellis was an intellectual companion as well as a housewife.

Even a political peace settled down about them. The War of Jenkins' Ear had been settled by treaty, and the colonists were free for a while of European wars and bloodshed. It would not last long, though. England and France were the two top rivals for dominance on land and sea and in colonial America. After eight years of armed conflict, they were still deadly rivals, and the treaty drawn up between them was no more than a breathing spell.

The French held territory all up the valleys of the Mississippi, Ohio, and St. Lawrence rivers. The Spanish held Florida, Mexico, and Cuba. The English owned territory stretching along the entire Atlantic seaboard from the border of Florida to the mouth of the St. Lawrence River, and around Hudson's Bay.

Friends were well-informed on world affairs; they corresponded back and forth with Friends and relatives in England and other parts of Europe; and many of them, especially in Philadelphia, were international merchants whose business would be affected by outbreaks of military hostilities in other countries and who kept in close touch with merchants abroad.

Benjamin Franklin's weekly paper, *The Pennsylvania Gazette, Containing the Freshest Advices Foreign and Domestick,* received correspondence from all over the world and reported it faithfully. Books and periodicals from Europe were available in the Philadelphia bookstores.

The greatest exchange of ideas among Friends occurred at Yearly Meeting, and in 1750, for the first time in his life, John Woolman had to consider the wisdom of going. Sarah was expecting a child and he did not want to leave her alone.

She knew how desperately he longed to go to Burlington and meet with the weighty Friends whom he did not see any other time.

"I ought not to leave thee."

"Thou must go. Yearly Meeting needs thee."

"Thou wilt be alone."

Sarah had to smile at that, because the statement was an exaggeration, and it came from a man who was in the habit of understating out of pure diffidence. She had a servant in the house to do the heavy work; there was a hired man on the grounds; she had relatives and neighbors close by.

"I shall be safe. Thou wilt be gone only a week."

He yielded to the gentle pressure and mounted his horse, glancing frequently back over his shoulder as he rode away.

Anthony Benezet was one of the first to clasp his hand. They had not seen each other in months and there was much to say. Anthony Benezet's concern over slavery was becoming as intense and forceful as his own.

"The Gentle Schoolmaster" was extending his tenderness and his love of teaching to the slaves. He was beginning a project that had never been tried in America before—a school for Negro children. The school was an added task he had taken on, in his own home, in his free time.

"These dark-skinned children learn as quickly as we," he assured John Woolman and everyone else to whom he talked. "I have found amongst them as great a variety of talents as amongst a like number of whites."

There could hardly have been anyone at Yearly Meeting who found the idea more stimulating than John Woolman did. Some scoffed, some doubted, some listened with reservation; but John Woolman believed Anthony Benezet's testimony, and it sharpened and pointed up his own faith.

He hurried home to give Sarah a complete account of all that had taken place at Yearly Meeting. There had been no minute on slavery this year, he said, but there had been much conversation and discussion about it among Friends between sessions.

Responsibilities never come singly. As Sarah's time of delivery approached, John Woolman was summoned home to Rancocas because his father had taken ill. He pushed his horse hard, because he could think of no worse possibility than small-pox. He did not, would not, could not want to see another member of his family die in such ugly misery.

Walking back into the main room of the house that he had been away from for so long, he felt rather biggish; the place and the room seemed smaller than it had when he was a boy. He climbed the enclosed staircase that turned at a right angle and followed his mother into the low-ceilinged bedroom.

The sight of his vigorous, farmer-strong father, a man of only sixty, confined to his bed, gave John Woolman another shock. This man with his head half buried in a feather pillow, his eyes glassy from fever, his horny hand limp and weak, had been someone upon whom he himself had depended through all of his life so far, and one glance told him that he could depend upon the older man no longer. It was his turn now to minister to his father.

He sat down beside the bed, grateful that Samuel Woolman's illness was at least not smallpox.

"How art thou?"

"This is my last sickness," came the reply.

"I had the fever once and recovered," John reminded him. His father did not want false encouragement. He knew what he knew. He wanted to talk to his son about his affairs, about the will that this same talented son had written for him, about the care of his wife after he was gone, and the launching into adult life of the remaining youngest of his brood. Eber and Abraham were only eleven and thirteen; Rachel was fifteen, and Jonah seventeen. And this oldest son—John—with his deep call to the ministry, needed one last piece of advice.

"The essay that thou didst write on slavery, John—"

John Woolman nodded.

"Thou must offer it to the Overseers of the Press."

John knew that his father was already so far spent that there was no hope of his recovery; but the older man's mind was entirely clear, and he said:

"I have all along been deeply affected with the oppression of the poor Negroes; and now, at last, my concern for them is as great as ever."

John promised that he would take his essay to the committee that handled the printing and publishing of Friends' literature.

"There have been many imperfections in my life," said Samuel Woolman. "Yet I know the power of Truth and I have tasted the love and goodness of God. I have no doubt that on leaving this life I shall enter a life more happy."

John stayed by his father's side until late in the night, long after the sick man had fallen asleep, and at last he tiptoed downstairs. There he found Asher, his mother, Esther and Jonah and Rachel. Twenty-two-year-old Uriah was apprenticed in Burlington, and the youngest two, Eber and Abraham, to tradesmen. All would be called home for this grave occasion.

Those at home sat in silence together, and none thought of rest, for any moment could be the last.

The next day a sister of Samuel Woolman's called and found him very weak.

"I hope," he told his sister, "that I shall shortly go to rest."

His physical strength continued to fail, until he lost consciousness altogether and slipped into his final sleep.

Again the burden of responsibility fell to John to settle affairs and distribute property, so that he dared not succumb to his grief. His mother was to remain at the farmhouse on the Rancocas, retaining title in "one half of the improvements, half the barn, half the orchards, half the marshes on both sides of the creek, with firewood and fencing to supply her said half. . . ."

Asher was to enjoy the remaining half and considerable farmland. All were remembered with money, or lands, or household effects. Bequests to the youngest were left in trust with older members. To John went one-third of a piece of land at Evesham, the other two portions going to Jonah and Asher.

At last all was tended to; his widowed mother left in the care of Asher, his father's will probated. John Woolman returned to his wife, his home, his orchards, and his shop on Mill Street.

No longer was Samuel Woolman *the* Woolman name in the Quaker community. The line of descent had passed on to the next, from Samuel to John. Barely thirty, John Woolman was now the representative to Quarterly and Yearly Meetings, the seasoned elder, the caller upon the sick, the owner of land, the head of a family.

The birth of his daughter, Mary, deepened his sense of maturity. How gradually but inevitably these responsibilities had come upon him one after another! As he knelt by the cradle and felt the tiny hand grasp his forefinger that December day, only nine weeks after his father's death, John Woolman felt a renewed concern for all of humanity. Here was all of humanity in this tiny person that he and Sarah had created. When it was given to man to create life, then it must also be given to man to protect and treasure it.

Shortly thereafter, he hunted among his papers for the essay that his father had felt possessed so much merit, "Some Considerations on the Keeping of Slaves." His sister had liked it; she had wept when he read it to her. He looked through it carefully once more, thought about it, and made a few corrections before taking it with him to next Yearly Meeting.

Meanwhile there were many things to take up a man's time and thoughts. His shop was prospering; his rich farmland was yielding good crops; and he was still a voracious reader and scholar. To be a worth-while citizen, to serve humanity, a man must know as much as possible about many subjects, especially those subjects that contained an implication of service, such as law and medicine. Wills, bills of sale, slavery, Indian treaties were legal problems. The community had long since learned that legal documents drawn by John Woolman held water, and he developed an actual law practice. He was even called upon occasionally to a task of surveying. Smallpox and fevers were medical problems. He had been calling upon the sick for years. Like Elizabeth Haddon Estaugh he knew the wild herbs and drugs and symptoms of the obvious diseases of the times; he had even acquired some skill in bleeding a patient.

Neighbors, friends, and an occasional stranger stopped at his shop and asked to have apprenticeship contracts prepared or a will drawn. Often sickness and will-drawing came out of the same situation.

"About this time a person at some distance lying sick, his brother came to me to write his will."

Woolman knew that the man owned slaves.

"What disposition dost thou plan to make of thy slaves?"

The question proved a little startling. Of course, they would be provided for in the will. They were valuable holdings. Further, just in case John Woolman was worried about the hands into which they would fall, they would be bequeathed to the sick man's own children.

Quiet, gentle, confident, John Woolman smiled. There was no longer any quicksand of indecision under his feet. His thinking was clear, his moral decisions spontaneous. Yet he did not want to offend a client.

"I really believe that the process of continuing slavery to these people is not right, and I have a scruple in my mind against doing writings of this kind."

In spite of Woolman's cautious approach, a spark of anger flashed in his visitor's eyes. This Woolman was becoming positively eccentric!

"See here. Thy writing is profitable to thee. If I pay thee a fee to write a document, the contents of the document do not concern thee."

Woolman nodded his head in agreement. Strictly speaking, the man was right. He replied again in an even more gentle voice.

"I know that many in our Society keep slaves, yet it makes me uneasy to be concerned with it, and I desire to be excused from writing the will."

The man made no reply. Frustrated into tight-lipped silence by this man who cared nothing for his fees, he strode abruptly out of the shop and down Mill Street, not once caring to glance backward.

II

THE TIDES OF WAR

John Woolman abhorred anger, even though he understood it, and he knew that arousing it in someone else defeated his own purposes. But there were times when a man had to stand firm regardless of the results. Usually John Woolman's approach to people was so gentle that it stirred a loving response where none had been thought to exist. Nowhere was this more evident than in the multitude of unrecorded visits that he made to homes in out-of-the-way places.

To families so widely separated from one another in a country that was still largely a wilderness, a visitor was an event; and when the visitor brought comforting words and a sustaining message with him, he was a blessing that could not be measured. John Woolman the boy had once yielded to John Woolman the saint, and the process was continuing as John

Woolman the minister was outstripping John Woolman the prosperous citizen. Families isolated from the central community prayed for his inspiring visits. He rode around the country seeking out the lonely as well as the sick whenever his shop and crops would permit, spending long hours with them in conversation, sitting with them in silent meditation, leaving behind him renewed courage and glowing hearts.

But a man cannot spend all of himself without retiring once in a while to renew his own resources. John Woolman was rarely absent from First Day Meeting for Worship, and there was no day that he did not set aside some time for religious reading and meditation.

His perspective had long since gone beyond his own community, as a result of his travels to the Southland, New York, Long Island, and New England; and as he read *The Pennsylvania Gazette* each week he was glad for the temporary peace that the colonies were enjoying, even though he knew, as many more did, that it was only nominal.

In 1751 and 1752 Benjamin Franklin could allow the first page of his four-page weekly to be devoted to a literary gem, a murder, or a lottery scheme to finish the steeple of Christ Church (Church of England) in Philadelphia. Once in a while he reprinted in toto an article from *The Gentleman's Magazine* of London that summed up the world news. His page 2 carried colonial news from Boston, New York, Williamsburg, and other cities; pages 3 and 4 were usually devoted to paid advertisements: a plantation or sawmill for sale; a newly imported shipload of merchandise offered for sale by one of the importers of the times, Mordecai Yarnall, Philip or Daniel Benezet, John Smith, Alexander Hamilton. Each issue carried its list of runaway slaves with exact descriptions so that they could be apprehended.

These items were a poor substitute for war news and they

were not likely to please John Woolman or any other orthodox Friend. Lotteries they placed beyond the pale. Slaves would not run away if they were happy with their lot.

Gradually symptoms of an impending war began to creep back into the *Gazette:* men-of-war being built at foreign ports for His Majesty's service; a note that the navy of this Kingdom is in a manner rebuilt since the late war; troop shipments; rumors that the French were building forts in the Ohio Valley.

By 1753 the French forts were a fact, on Pennsylvania's western flank and elsewhere. Those dwelling in the English colonies all up and down the Atlantic seaboard knew that the deadly rivalry between France and England for control of North America would surely break out again. It was really a rivalry for world power—expanding England versus the other countries of the world. The British Empire was spreading out everywhere, even in far-off India, where the East India Company was penetrating one princely state after another, bringing home wealth to the mother country.

The Pennsylvania Assembly was in Quaker control, and the Quakers were as fixed as ever in their determination to live at peace with whatever neighbors destiny brought them. Force of arms was not their way. But they were not the only people in Pennsylvania any more, and theirs was not the only party in the Assembly. With the French and the Indians threatening the western borders of Virginia, Pennsylvania, and New York, the stand the Quakers took against military preparedness seemed very shortsighted to many.

John Woolman went anxiously to Philadelphia to the Yearly Meeting in 1753, and his anxiety was no less when Yearly Meeting was over. He sought out Peter Andrews, Anthony Benezet, and weighty Friends from England. The world situation impressed them all the same way. Their opinions dovetailed. War between the great powers was surely brewing.

The English colonies gingerly hugged the coast and made no effort to push westward because the wilderness offered no means of travel except the streams and rivers, and the wilderness was still peopled with Indians. The French had erected a fort at the point where the Allegheny and the Monongahela rivers unite to form the Ohio and had named it Fort Duquesne. The French were gradually winning the friendship and allegiance of the Indians.

Scheduled Yearly Meeting sessions met as scheduled, and the members of the Society sat down to worship and transact business together as they had in generations past with persecutors knocking at their doors. It was their stolid, unshakable persistence of continuing along the straight line they had marked out for themselves that so often infuriated the hasty, the impatient, or the violently inclined who tried to deal with them.

Slavery was the gnawing, persistent concern of those Friends who were agitating for its abolition at Yearly Meeting of ninth month, 1753. (The calendar was revised about this time, and January was made the first month of the year; so ninth month now means September.) Year after year Friends had groped for an answer that would receive the unanimous support of the group. Love and unity must continue among Friends, or the whole significance of their faith would be lost.

John Woolman experienced a little twinge of joy when he heard the report of the Overseers of the Press (Anthony Benezet had been appointed to that committee a year earlier). Israel Pemberton, scholar and exquisite penman, recording clerk of the Meeting, carefully wrote his minute:

"The Overseers of the Press acquainted the Meeting that besides several treatises before mentioned they now have under consideration a short one containing 'Considerations Concerning the Keeping of Negroes' by John Woolman, which will be soon printed and ready to distribute to the several Quarterly Meetings."

If his writings could be acceptable to the Society, that would be one more way in which he could reach Friends with his message. John Woolman decided that he would write other pieces, and he prayed fervently that his pen would be guided and gifted enough to serve this great intent.

"I wrote that essay so long ago, I have further ideas upon the subject now," he told Sarah when he returned to Mount Holly.

As they sat and talked it over, the idea of an epistle addressed to the next Yearly Meeting seemed like the best approach. Friends liked to write thoughtful epistles to one another. Each year the Yearly Meetings exchanged epistles containing news of their activities, encouragement if it was needed, and hopes for the future. Groups were usually designated to write the various epistles that went out to London, Maryland, Virginia, Long Island, New England. Anyone with a gifted pen was apt to be called upon to serve on an epistle committee, and each year Friends waited eagerly for the reading of the epistles from far-off places.

"There is a whole year in which to write it," Sarah reminded him.

When he told her that his essay was to be sent to Benjamin Franklin's printing shop for publication, she was not surprised. Then she could add:

"Thou dost write well."

"Beloved wife," were words that John Woolman used often to Sarah at home or to Sarah in letters when he was on a journey.

Sarah, his beloved wife, was going to give him another child, before another Yearly Meeting time could roll around.

Early in 1754 the rumors were confirmed that the previous

autumn the governor of Virginia had sent an inexperienced young surveyor, George Washington, to Fort Duquesne with a message to the French that they withdraw from what were unquestionably English lands. The French did not consider the lands unquestionably English, and the commandant at the fort returned Washington to the governor of Virginia with a reply that he had instructions from *his* king to keep possession, to advance farther, and to fight any that should oppose him. As a matter of fact, the commandant told Mr. Washington, he was surprised the English had not already attacked, because he had been expecting an English army to do so for the past twelve months.

The Quakers continued their aloof attitude toward military matters.

During the spring and summer of that year, John Woolman was deeply distracted by personal problems. A constant prayer flowed through his being for the health of his wife, who was not carrying this second child as easily as the first. He became more solicitous of her than before. He arose before the sun each morning to look to his farmer's chores, then walked into town to attend to his shop and his tailoring assignments. His shop was beginning to take more time than he cared to give it. Upon letting himself in he looked around at his stock of goods. He carried no frivolous lines, yet there were on his shelves so many items that people only thought they needed and that they could really do without.

He had barely settled to his sewing when a customer entered, ready to list off a great quantity of proposed purchases.

"I shall give thee some of them but not all," Woolman told him.

"Thou hast the other articles."

"Yes, but thou canst not afford them, and I do not intend to let thee go into needless debt."

It was the custom of the times to buy on credit.

Still Woolman's trade increased week after week, because the world beats a path to the door of an honest shopkeeper.

Prosperity in and of itself was one of Woolman's personal problems, and he seriously considered discontinuing some of the lines of merchandise. He needed more time for meditation, for inner silence, for visiting families that needed ministerial service, for completing his epistle on slavery, for sitting with his wife during these remaining months of her pregnancy, for praying that somehow war might be averted. War news continually crowded in upon his thinking.

The Woolman that existed within himself and in whom the spirit of God functioned so fully continued through life as sensitive and tender as the small boy who had responded so much more deeply than all of his brothers and sisters to the Meetings for Worship, to the family readings, to any gentle remonstrance. His spiritual self had matured and expanded over the years without losing any of its naive perceptiveness. And so, when he lay down at night to sleep and closed his eyes for that last moment of conscious awareness of the divine spirit, the Quaker "Light," his concerns lived on in his dreams.

He dreamed one night that he was walking in an orchard, in the middle of the afternoon, when two lights appeared in the east that looked like two suns. But they were overcast and gloomy.

"In a few minutes the air in the East appeared to be mingled with fire and like a terrible storm coming westward the streams of fire reached the orchard where I stood, but I felt no harm," he described it later in his *Journal*.

As the streams of fire swept around him, he discovered an acquaintance at his side. The acquaintance was deeply disturbed and alarmed by the phenomenon, but Woolman felt only a deep calm, and he said:

"We must all once die, and if it please the Lord that our death be in this way, it's good for us to be resigned."

His dream continued, and in it he walked to a house nearby and going upstairs found "people with sad and troubled aspects." He went on to the next room, whose floor was of loose boards, and sat down alone near an open window. Outside, the phenomenon of his dream went on: three great red streams in the south stretching from the earth to the clouds, and, crisscrossing them, other streams of red.

As he continued to watch out of the window, the land before him became a green plain, and on it stood "in military posture" a great quantity of men. They were going through a military drill, and as they passed under Woolman's window they looked up and scoffed and taunted him. The old captain of militia himself walked up and told Woolman:

"These men are assembled to improve in the discipline of war."

John Woolman awoke, staring about him in the darkened bedchamber. Beside him Sarah slept quietly and undisturbed.

In what a vivid way had God chosen to speak to him! He could still see the vision against the background of darkness, the glowing red sky and the vivid green ground, the marching soldiers and their mocking faces.

Carefully he slid out of bed and groped his way downstairs, where he found a candle and held its tip against the remaining embers of the fire. Then he went to his writing table with the candle and drew a rough sketch of the scene before it could crumble away, dissolving from memory the way dreams will.

But he never forgot that dream. It was too sinister an omen.

He carried it with him in the back of his mind into the summer.

News soon reached the Delaware Valley folk that George Washington had led a military attack against the French in the Ohio Valley and had met with disastrous defeat at Fort Necessity, some forty miles from Fort Duquesne. Woolman felt a deep grief for the many-sided mistake. Now the Indians knew that the English were weak and the French strong. Now the scattered English settlers on the frontiers could expect serious trouble from the Indians.

"Now men will really assemble to improve in the discipline of needless and fruitless war," was Woolman's solemn reflection.

He held in his hand the July 25, 1754, issue of Benjamin Franklin's paper. It contained the complete terms of surrender. He tried not to let his mood of depression show too plainly.

He was sitting at Sarah's bedside where she lay still weakened by the recent birth of his son. The tiny boy was weak, too; he had come into the world delicate, striving for life, needing every ounce of care and love and prayer that anyone could give him if he was to survive.

Sarah turned her head toward her husband and held out her hand. He took her hand in his.

"John . . ."

"Beloved . . ."

Sarah needed encouragement. She must have first call on his attention. He must dismiss from his mind these outside distractions. His son must live and grow. But the outside distractions would not be dismissed. His son would grow up into a world at war, if those who knew the formula for peace relaxed their vigilance.

A tiny cry from the cradle sharpened Woolman's resolve.

A man must face what must be faced, and he must accept what God determines will be. He must somehow find the time for all of his problems both within his home and on the outside.

Sarah had not heard the baby cry. She had closed her eyes and slipped into a light sleep. Woolman let go of her hand and tiptoed away from her side. When he was alone he could only bow his head on his hands and endeavor to place his utmost faith in Divine Judgment at the possibilities ahead of him: loss of his son, maybe loss of his wife, loss of his Quaker world if the tides of war swept over it.

In August the *Pennsylvania Gazette* reported warlike preparations in the Southern colonies. The House of Burgesses of Virginia was not a Quaker body, and it bristled more readily than the Pennsylvania Assembly when the question of military defense against the French came up. That summer it levied a poll tax of "two shillings per poll on December 10 next, and three shillings or thirty pounds of tobacco the last day of July next," to "protect His Majesty's subjects in this colony against insults and encroachments of the French."

Woolman wanted particularly to finish his epistle on slavery even though he realized that the problems of war would have to be considered at Yearly Meeting. If hostility between the French and English actually did break out, the Friends would have many grave questions to answer.

Sarah had recovered her strength by the time of Yearly Meeting, but her health was still too fragile for traveling. A long horseback ride or wagon ride would have been out of the question.

"I hesitate to leave thee," said Woolman, looking at her and at the baby that continued so weak. Sarah urged him to go. After all, the Meeting this year would be in nearby Burlington. She knew how anxious he was to present his epistle, and how much the sessions depended upon his weight and eloquence.

Torn between two needs, John Woolman at last decided to make the trip. If his son's health took a turn for the worse, a fast rider could reach him in Burlington with the news in a few hours, and he could return home as quickly.

Friends of the Yearly Meeting for the Provinces of Pennsylvania and New Jersey who gathered in the first week of September, 1754, had had time to read "Some Considerations on the Keeping of Negroes," and they came together with no small eagerness hoping to hear from its author. He was personal minister to many. He was the voice of many more.

John Woolman's "Epistle of Caution and Advice Concerning the Buying and Keeping of Slaves" was not the revealing of a sudden secret. He had discussed it with many while he labored on it. When Anthony Benezet stood up to read the epistle, a subdued excitement spread over the gathering.

"Dear Friends: It hath frequently been the Concern of our Yearly Meeting to testify their uneasiness and disunity with the importation and purchasing of Negroes and other slaves, and to direct the Overseers of the several Meetings to advise and deal with such as engage therein.

"The characteristic and badge of a true Christian is love and good works; our Saviour's whole life on earth was one continual exercise of them; Love one another, says He, as I have loved you. How can we be said to love our brethren who bring, or for selfish ends keep them in bondage? . . .

"Finally brethren we entreat you in the bowels of Gospel Love seriously to weigh the cause of detaining them in bondage. . . ."

The Meeting plunged into a deep silence after hearing Woolman's epistle, which had probed to the core of the issue. At length the decision came—to send the epistle in the name of the Yearly Meeting to the other Yearly Meetings in America. Its incendiary contents were to circulate all over the continent. The significance of its impact would not be measurable for years to come.

Its full text was to be included in the Yearly Meeting minutes, and since the minutes were written in longhand, the letter occupied three pages. The fact that his name did not appear on the letter as author did not worry Woolman. Meeting epistles never carried an author's name. What was more important, this epistle on slavery was going out as an official advice from the largest and most influential Quaker community in the New World. It would be read at Yearly, Quarterly, and Monthly Meetings, north and south, and to it were attached the signatures of twelve well-known Quaker names.

Overjoyed at this extraordinary progress toward unity on the evil of slavery, and realizing that this progress could be advanced still further at future meetings, John Woolman bade good-by to Anthony Benezet and others with a considerable feeling of excitement and hurried home.

His excitement had to be throttled to a minimum when he reached his house, because Sarah welcomed him with frightened eyes.

"The baby has grown weaker," she began, and her voice broke.

Together they sat by the tiny bed and watched life ebb away.

John Woolman's only son had lived a mere two months and ten days.

12

A PEACEABLE PEOPLE

Now faith was a refuge, indeed; and John Woolman needed every ounce of it in accepting the tragedy of this baby's death. He looked anxiously at Mary, almost four, and hoped that her bouncing, mischievous health would endure, that she would not suddenly fade and disappear from his life, or be snatched away by a mysterious fever or the smallpox.

"We must give thanks in everything," he reminded himself. "God's vision is infinite, and only He can see the wisdom in my son's death."

Through the balance of the winter he and Sarah sought solace in their work, and on First Day mornings they traveled through the snow to Meeting, knowing their grief would find healing in the communal silence.

John Woolman searched his heart for continued messages

on slavery to further the progress that had already been made in the hearts of Friends. More frequently than in the past those who could not quite surrender the luxury of slave service in their lifetimes were at least freeing them in their wills. Twice more Friends came to Woolman to write their wills and attempted to persuade him to provide for perpetuation of servitude for their Negroes.

"An ancient man of good esteem" was what Woolman called the neighbor who came to his house and asked him to write his will.

"I know thou hast young Negroes," Woolman observed before picking up his quill. "How dost thou purpose to dispose of them?"

The reply was not to Woolman's taste, for he went on, "I cannot write thy will without breaking my own peace."

The man went away, not too surprised by his experience; for by that time everyone who knew Woolman or knew of Woolman knew Woolman's views on slavery. The man knew more than that about Woolman: he knew his writing skill and his knowledge of the law. It would be a better will if Woolman were to write it. In a few days he returned to have the will drawn.

"I have decided to liberate my slaves as you direct," he said.

This was the kind of joyful gratification upon which Woolman could subsist. To kindle a right spirit in another man's heart—was there any greater source of happiness?

Within a very short time the episode was repeated.

Another neighbor had met with an injury, and Woolman was called to his bedside because of his knowledge of practical medicine. Bleeding was a medical technique of the times, and Woolman was skillful in it.

"A neighbor received a bad bruise in his body and sent for

me to bleed him, which being done he desired me to write his will."

Woolman took out a piece of paper to make notes while the man told him how he wanted his properties distributed and to which of his children he wanted a slave bequeathed. Woolman knew the pain and discomfort the man was in, and so he did not argue with him then. He went quietly home, wrote all of the will except the clause about the slave, and returned the next day. He found the patient a little stronger after his night's sleep, and he read the uncompleted document to him.

"I cannot write any instrument by which my fellow creatures are made slaves without bringing trouble to my own mind," he said at the end in the kindliest, friendliest tone of voice he could command.

The sick man smiled weakly, and he and Woolman talked for a long time about the immorality of slavery. At length he agreed to set his slave free, and Woolman went home once more to finish the will.

"Deep rooted customs, though wrong, are not easily altered; but it is the duty of all to be firm in that which they certainly know is right for them," was Woolman's tolerant observation.

When slavery ended in each human heart it would be ended forever. How many hearts would God appoint him to reach in his lifetime? A little twinge of personal ambition clouded his thinking, and it embarrassed him. He must be more cautious of his own weakness to vanity; he must discipline himself carefully; he must guard against ever being a spokesman for himself.

No one can live in a world where slavery is part of the pattern and not be tainted by it. Woolman was the executor of a will that required the disposition of a nine-year-old boy. His heart sickened when he realized that having accepted the responsibility long ago he must now fulfill the legal requirements of the document and arrange for the sale of a child. He made the best of a bad situation and placed the lad with a gentle and sympathetic master. The boy could not have his freedom until he was thirty, not for another twenty-one years; and the evil deed haunted Woolman's conscience for all the rest of his life, in spite of the crowding in upon him and his Quaker world of the bitter conflict between France and England for dominance of America.

The problems of money for war materials, conscription, taxes, Indian raids presented themselves in rapid succession, because they were all part of the same problem: war. By the middle of summer the colonies knew that war was upon them even though it had not been officially declared, because news of General Braddock's humiliating defeat at Fort Duquesne spread gloom over the Atlantic seaboard.

England had dispatched Edward Braddock and a complement of troops to Virginia, and from there he was to be commander in chief of all forces raised in the New World. After a conference with the governors of Virginia, North Carolina, Maryland, Pennsylvania, New York, and Massachusetts, General Braddock decided that he would attack the French at their vital points: Crown Point on Lake Champlain, Fort Niagara on the St. Lawrence River, and Fort Duquesne in western Pennsylvania. So important did he consider the recapture of Fort Duquesne that he chose to command that expedition himself.

But Braddock was not a colonial, and he did not understand colonial life or the Indians. Colonials did not make good soldiers, he was sure, and for Indian scouts he felt only frank contempt. He could have captured Fort Duquesne had he been able to adapt his thinking to the environment, because his forces were fresher than and far outnumbered the

French and Indians. When he met them at the Monongahela, he at first put the enemy to rout; but he made the mistake of keeping his solid formations. The French and Indians broke ranks and took shelter behind trees, shrubs, and rocks; and they found the solidly massed soldiers in their brilliant red coats easy targets. Braddock, a majority of his officers, and more than half of his men were killed, and the entire expedition defeated.

What little respect the Ohio Indians had left for the English vanished when Braddock was defeated; and what faith the colonial people had in the mother country for protection sank to a new low. It was then that they began to think of themselves as a separate people who must look after their own affairs. Perhaps they ought to have their own defenses and their own militia. Benjamin Franklin's recent suggestion that the colonies unite to form a single militia common to all was not without merit.

Two months after Braddock's defeat Friends packed their saddlebags and rode with grim and sober faces toward Yearly Meeting in Philadelphia: the Woolmans, the Willses, the Smiths, the Yarnalls, the Pembertons, the Penningtons, the Morrises, the Benezets, John Churchman, Samuel Fothergill from London, Isaac Andrews. Peter Andrews was in England.

Some of their thinking on the question of war and its involvements had already been resolved, because their ministers and elders had met in the spring and had sent out an epistle "To Friends on the continent of America." "We have found it to be our duty to cease from those national contests productive of misery and bloodshed . . ."

That epistle had been signed by John Woolman, Mordecai Yarnall, John Churchman, William Morris, Isaac Andrews, and nine other of the weightiest names in American Quakerdom, and during the summer, before and after Braddock's defeat, it had circulated throughout the "continent of America."

John Woolman wondered if there had ever been as significant a Yearly Meeting as this was bound to be.

The city of Philadelphia was buzzing with politics, with news of Indian atrocities less than a hundred miles to the west, with strong rumors that the French and Indians were planning to invade Pennsylvania, and with tensions caused by the refusal of the large Quaker block in the Assembly to appropriate funds for war purposes. The opposition, the party of the Proprietors, was trying to unite the anti-Quaker groups. During the years after William Penn's death, the Proprietorship had passed to a group of men who were not as great as he, men whose faith in Quakerism was not as deep.

To John Woolman, who saw Truth so much more clearly than other men, there could be no compromising with or rationalizing of the issue of militarism. If a man, because of his religious convictions, considered himself a pacifist, then not only did he not serve in the armed forces, but he did not lend his wagons to carry military supplies or pay taxes to finance military campaigns. If Friends compromised on these issues they "might approach so near to fighting that the distinction would be little else but the name of a peaceable people."

Thus Friends found themselves disunited on the war question as well as on the slavery question. In the Philadelphia Yearly Meeting sessions, as in the Assembly, some sincerely felt that defense against attack was reasonable. Should a war tax be levied, some planned to pay it, some planned to refuse.

The moral question of supporting even a defensive war was not resolved immediately, and the Friends appointed two committees to consider it further. One committee was to correspond with Friends in London; the other was to take up the problem with the Monthly and Quarterly Meetings under the jurisdiction of the Philadelphia Yearly Meeting.

"Peter Andrews is in England now," said John Woolman with great confidence. "When our letters arrive, he will be present at the discussion."

The Friends did not lose their perspective in spite of the fact that worldly problems pressed so closely upon them. When they had accomplished as much as they could on the war question, they went on to the next, a report from a committee that had been designated to consider the Queries.

Queries? Just a list of questions for the individual member to ponder in his quest for Truth. Believing in the absolute right of each individual to make his own moral decisions and work out his own relationships with God, the Friends had no rules worded "Thou shalt" or "Thou shalt not," but just a series of questions based on the faith that were read at regular intervals in Monthly Meeting, so that the individual could listen and ponder and silently search his own soul. Over the years Friends have developed an extraordinary capacity for honest self-appraisal.

At the beginning of the several days' sessions, a special committee had been appointed to work over the Queries and recommend revisions and additions. Samuel Fothergill, John Woolman, John Churchman, Samuel Smith, Isaac Andrews, and eight others had done a careful job, but John Woolman was secretly disappointed with one of the Queries— slavery. Yet, no matter how deeply he felt on it, he did not have the right to disrupt the unity of the group by trying to force a decision that they were not ready to make.

A committee member stood up to read the revised Queries.

1. Are all meetings for religious worship and discipline duly attended, the hour observed, and are Friends preserved from

sleeping or any other indecent behavior therein, particularly from chewing tobacco or taking snuff?

2. Is love and unity maintained amongst you as becomes brethren? Are talebearing, backbiting, and evil reports discouraged, and where any differences arise are endeavors used speedily to end them?

3. Are Friends careful to bring up those under their direction in plainness of speech, behavior, and approval, in frequent readings of the Holy Scriptures, to restrain them from reading pernicious books and the corrupt conversation of the world?

4. Are Friends careful to avoid the excessive use of spirituous liquors . . . ?

5. Are poor Friends' necessities duly inspected . . . ?

6. Do no young or single persons make proposals of marriage with each other without consent of parents or guardians . . . ?

8. Do you maintain faithful testimony against taking or administering oaths, the payment of priests' wages or church rates . . . bearing of arms, training or military services . . . ? [English Friends refused to take oaths, and many Friends still do, because of the instruction in the New Testament to "swear not at all," and because they believe there ought to be only one level of truth-telling which makes oaths unnecessary. They refused to pay tithes to support the Church of England, and incurred a great deal of persecution as a result.]

9. Are Friends careful to make their wills and settle their outward estates whilst in health . . . ?

10. *Are Friends clear of importing or buying Negroes and do they use those well which they are possessed of by inheritance or otherwise, endeavoring to train them up in the principles of the Christian religion?*

11. Are Friends careful to live within the bounds of their circumstances and to avoid launching into trade and business beyond their ability to manage; are they punctual to their promises and just in the payment of their debts . . . ?

Tension slowly gathered and mounted throughout the reading of the Queries, and reached its maximum on Query Number 10. When it was apparent that they had not taken a clear-cut position, the tension eased, and Woolman relaxed with a twinge of discouragement.

"It *was* progress, I suppose," said John to Sarah afterward, trying to reassure himself and to shake off his discouragement at the same time. "The old Query on slavery merely said, 'Do Friends observe the former advice of our Yearly Meeting not to encourage the importation of Negroes nor to buy them after imported?' "

Sarah nodded her understanding. She need not offend him by counseling patience; he was his own best counselor on that.

John Woolman returned to Philadelphia in November, because the two committees appointed to consider the payment of a war tax held a special meeting at the Penn Charter School. Rush of events had forced them to do so. The Pennsylvania Assembly was in session, and the governor and his proprietors were pleading for special legislation.

War was spreading and to the advantage of the French from Nova Scotia to Virginia. Massachusetts, Connecticut, and other New England colonies were raising troops; so was Virginia. Virginia troops under George Washington were assuming almost full responsibility for the safety of the western frontiers of Pennsylvania and Virginia, and the farmers of those frontiers were beginning to get a taste of the kind of Indian warfare with which New England had been familiar for a long time. There had been a big raid on Penn's Creek settlement just the previous month.

Governor Morris was arguing with the Assembly for a militia law and funds for military equipment, but he would not allow them to levy a real estate tax, since the Proprietors were the biggest landowners.

Gathered in another building in the same city, the Friends' two committees drafted a letter to Friends in the Assembly cautioning them that many Friends would decline, at whatever penalty to themselves, to pay a war tax. "It is our fervent desire that you may be enabled to secure peace and tranquility to yourselves and those you represent by pursuing measures consistent with our peaceable principles."

Friends in public office recognized quickly enough the weight of the names that signed that letter; some were their own blood kin; in some instances their thinking was in complete accord and they did not need to have the "peaceable principles" explained to them.

But John Woolman was grieved as he sat with the other committee members in the schoolhouse. He was grieved because he was a purist, a man who thought so purely and in such a clear way that he could not understand compromise. The committee members were divided. They had managed to agree on the message to the Assembly, but the constraint was severe, and only their Quaker training held them from open quarrel.

"Shall we unite in silent worship?" suggested one.

Yes. That was the proper way to begin—united—and then proceed to the discussion of the peace testimony.

Woolman watched them begin—tight-lipped. He was tight-lipped himself. As the discussion developed, one spoke after another, some favoring the support of a defensive war, others opposing. Each time a Friend affirmed his peaceable principles John Woolman's hope was raised, but he began to see, as everyone else did, that the committee could not unite. A disunited Friends' group could not recommend any course of action.

After an intense period of striving, the Friends who favored compromise got to their feet.

"We think it best to withdraw from the Meeting."

None detained them. It was the only way. When they were gone from the room, those who remained, the absolute pacifists, John Woolman among them, sat a long time with bowed heads and pained hearts. The new tax was legal, and the law carried penalties. Once again their faith must bear the test of official reprisal, as it had generations before in both England and America.

When God spoke to a man's heart, a man had no scruple but to obey. To this end the remaining committee members composed another letter, addressed to their own Monthly and Quarterly Meetings: "As we cannot be concerned in wars and fighting so neither ought we to contribute thereto by paying the tax directed by the said act, though suffering be the consequence of our refusal. . . ."

They parted company from one another with heavy hearts, not really knowing what the future held in store for them.

"It was a conference the most weighty that ever I was at," was John Woolman's conclusion.

The Assembly did finally pass a bill to raise money from taxes. It passed a militia bill, too, but only for voluntary enlistment; the bill specifically exempted Friends and other conscientious objectors. "Whereas the Province was first settled by Quakers," it stated, "to compel them to bear arms would be a direct breach of our charter of privileges."

John Woolman made a dutiful report to his own Monthly Meeting, and the lines of the members' faces deepened as he talked.

Fresh news of Indian atrocities kept coming in from the frontiers: houses burned, inhabitants scalped, murdered, or kidnaped. And the news was used in every way to excite men into enlisting in the militia. Dead bodies of three frontiersmen were dragged through the streets of Philadelphia in open wagons, their heads raw where the scalps had been torn off, while crowds followed after the wagons shouting curses against the Indians, crying for reprisals, and shrieking insults at Quakers for not joining in the war.

13

"A LOVE CLOTHES MY MIND"

After nearly a hundred years of peaceful living in the Delaware Valley the Friends were approaching another crisis. It could mean that they would be persecuted as they once had been. Their lands or property could be seized for fines and unpaid taxes. Such things happened to a people who refused to obey the laws that conflicted with their faith.

There is only one supreme law: the will of God speaking in a man's heart, the Friends' Inner Light, that supersedes all the laws of men. A man's first obligation in the scheme of things is to be right with God. George Fox, the founder of the Society, had first called its members Children of Light.

The Light in John Woolman's heart that had begun as a tiny spark in boyhood grew stronger with each passing year, until, in the years of great decision for the Society of Friends, when he was in his middle and late thirties, his Light illuminated his whole personality, kindled the spark in other hearts, clarified the thinking of countless Friends, and guided John Woolman himself forward in an unswerving line. What was his final goal? He neither knew nor thought he had the right to ask. He understood only that he must follow the bidding of the voice that spoke so persistently within him and to which he surrendered himself with greater and greater ease.

It bade him give more time to visiting families, writing letters, traveling around the countryside as a visiting minister at other meetings. It bade him reason with those who were not clear in their thinking.

"We treat our slaves well," slaveowners would argue, and Woolman would nod patiently. "We are loyal subjects of His Most Sacred Majesty," advocates of a war tax would say. Or, "We *are* in great danger from the French and Indians. Surely a defensive war is justifiable."

He listened with deep understanding and profound sympathy. It took strong faith to make a decision that could cost one one's freedom and comfort.

"Several letters from London in which mention is made that war with France seems inevitable though the French are letting the English take their vessels without reprisals," Benjamin Franklin reported in his paper early in January.

Feelings ran higher and higher in the English colonies against the French and Indians, and in April, 1756, Governor Robert Hunter Morris actually issued a declaration of war against the Delaware tribe and others in confederacy with them. Governor Morris knew better than to expect the Quaker legislature to support such a measure; so he and his council published the proclamation without any advance warning. It offered one hundred fifty Spanish dollars or pieces of eight for each male Indian above the age of twelve brought in as a captive and one hundred thirty pieces of eight for the scalp of each male Indian over twelve. There was a list of prices that would be paid for the scalps of women and children.

Sensible of the terrible long-range perils of such a barbarous policy, knowing that atrocities only lead to the atrocities of reprisal to the end of time, weighty Friends doubled and redoubled their efforts for peace. Some sent a protest directly to the governor. Great numbers of them attended the Spring Meeting of Ministers and Elders in Philadelphia to labor together to influence Friends to support their own peace testimony. Some resigned from their seats in the Assembly.

"A day to be remembered through many generations with sorrow," wrote Samuel Fothergill. "The governor agreed to proclaim war against the Delawares and delivered the hatchet into the hands of some of the Indians."

Two weeks after the declaration of war upon the Indians John Woolman went to Monthly Meeting at Burlington with an aching heart.

"I have drawings on my mind to visit Friends on Truth's account on Long Island and thereabouts," he told them, and they understood that he wanted to carry his concern for peace and love to other meetings. He was not alone in his longing to commune with others. At the same Meeting Abraham Farrington expressed a desire to visit Friends on Truth's account in some of the countries of Europe. The Meeting granted certificates to both men.

John Woolman set out during the next few days. Customers could come knocking at the door of his shop for merchandise which they did not need; half-finished jackets and coats could wait; even his orchards could await his return for their "hoeing, grafting, trimming, and inoculating."

"When I reached the island I lodged the first night at the house of my dear friend Richard Hallett," says John Woolman's *Journal*.

Richard Hallett, nearly thirty years older than Woolman, was himself a minister, and when he flung open his door to welcome his visitor his eyes filmed over with joy. His New Town Meeting needed John Woolman's message.

"The next day being the first day of the week, I was at the Meeting in New Town, in which we experienced the renewed manifestations of the love of Jesus Christ to the comfort of the honest-hearted."

John Woolman remounted his horse.

"I went that night to Flushing. . . ."

Flushing Meeting House, still standing on Northern Boulevard, still a place of worship, was the home of the New York Yearly Meeting for years. George Fox himself had visited this Meeting on his visit to America in 1671 and had found it "A very large meeting, many hundreds of people being there." John Woolman, eighty-five years after Fox's visit, added his name to the list of great ministers who have visited Flushing. He attended Yearly Meeting and individual Meetings for Worship on Long Island. He found many Friends on Long Island who honored their faith in their daily living, but many more grieved him and to them he spoke with compassion.

"Many, I fear, are too much clogged with things of this life."

If their failing was to temporize on military activities, he reasoned with them on that. If he discovered them keeping slaves, he pleaded with them that slavery was a practice inconsistent with the purity of the Christian religion, a kind of worldliness, a desire for ease and comfort, and such greeds led to war.

The Monthly Meeting in the Meeting House at Westbury "ye 26th day of ye 5th month 1756" recorded his visit: "John Woolman produced a certificate from the Monthly Meeting of Friends at Burlington signifying their unity with him in this his religious visit, which was read to satisfaction, and he further desiring a few lines from us to Friends from whence he came, which this Meeting is free to give, and accordingly orders a certificate to be drawn against the next Monthly Meeting."

The meetings were deeply affected by his visit; and, seeing the courage of so many renewed, John Woolman could not help but realize that the pressures and problems of the times made an increased ministry necessary.

He journeyed back to Mount Holly, allowing his horse an easy gait so that he could reflect upon all that he had observed. Increased ministry, more ministers traveling to more meetings with greater frequency, to keep faith alive and forever renewed—that was his conclusion.

The Quaker faith teaches the personal responsibility of each individual. Not, what ought you to do? Nor, what ought to be done? But, what must I do?

"Too much of my time is given to worldly gain when I am needed in the ministry," was John Woolman's conclusion.

Accordingly, he closed the door of his retail shop forever. His earnings as a tailor, together with the produce of his farmlands, would be sufficient for himself and Sarah and Mary.

His decision did not come a minute too soon, because in the same month that Woolman made his journey to the Long Island Meetings the King of England went before both Houses of Parliament to read his declaration of war against France.

This, then, was total war, engulfing both Europe and America, but in America it was really the bitter rivalry between Great Britain and France for the control of the continent rich in natural resources.

The Quakers of Pennsylvania and New Jersey did not change their views or their efforts. They never stopped working for peace. The king's declaration simply made official what had been a fact for many months. The Quakers followed the same course they had been following right along: conferring with the Indians.

They had already held a four-day conference at the home of Israel Pemberton with some of the Delawares and agreed that a bigger conference was needed.

"We will pay the expenses," they told the governor of Pennsylvania.

That much pleased the governor, and he invited the Delaware chieftains to a conference, or peace treaty, at Easton, Pennsylvania.

Teedyuscung, king of the Delawares, had appointments for a great many conferences: at Niagara to chat with the French about providing food for his people, who were suffering from dislocation and war privations; at Onondaga, New York, where the Six Nations (powerful tribes of New York State and the Great Lakes Region) were conferring with the English.

At last Teedyuscung reached Easton, and he was no small figure of a man. He was tall and strong and angular, a gaudy dresser; he walked with a swagger and boasted in loud tones that he was truly a man, one who could drink a gallon of rum without getting drunk. With him came more than twenty of his picked warriors. The Delawares made a terrifying spectacle for the Indian-scared residents of Easton. Some of the Delawares had shirts made of checkered tablecloths that looked suspiciously as though they had been stolen from frontier cabins.

Teedyuscung was delighted to find Quakers at the conference.

"Now I believe all I have heard to be true!" he announced. Perhaps this was a genuine peace conference after all.

The governor was annoyed at this. And he was annoyed

again when he learned that four of Pennsylvania's weightiest Friends went to Teedyuscung's quarters and paid him a call. The courtesy touched the chieftain deeply, but the governor was ruffled, because rivalry between himself and the Quakers was still the order of the day. When the Quakers said peace, they meant total peace, and the governor wanted military help from the Delawares.

Teedyuscung was as shrewd a man as the governor. He wanted a few guarantees for his people. Both the French and the English coveted the lands of the Indians, he reminded the conference. Would the English guarantee the territory in the Susquehanna and Ohio Valleys to the Indians? If so, the Indians would join up with the English instead of the French.

The English were not so sure about that point, and the results of the conference were inconclusive; but English and Indians did part in friendship with promises of future conferences, and the Delawares went home loaded with gifts.

It was progress, but there would have to be many more conferences between Indians and English during the next few years before real peace could be achieved. This colonial war between England and France was more widespread than any of the other colonial wars, and there were many more tribes involved than the Ohio and Susquehanna Delawares.

Again a personal grief distracted Woolman when he was working along with the rest of the Friends to promote peace and ease the sufferings of the frontier dwellers. News reached him that Peter Andrews had died in England.

He had lost a part of himself, a mirror to his own thoughts, a source of strength, a friend who was closer to him than his own brothers. Peter Andrews had been a part of his life, an intimate part of his thinking and believing.

When he met with William Morris, John Churchman, Israel Pemberton, and many others who made up the new Meeting for Sufferings, he wanted Peter Andrews to be there. Peter Andrews could not be there; Peter Andrews was no more. John Woolman had to lay aside another personal grief and consider the service to be rendered to the living.

He forced himself to think of the concerns of this committee of twenty-odd, the Meeting for Sufferings, chosen to consider ways and means of easing the sufferings of frontier settlers. Money that was not paid in taxes could be contributed for peaceable purposes instead.

The London Yearly Meeting had created a Meeting for Sufferings more than eighty years earlier, when English Friends were enduring severe persecutions. Its duty had been to record the sufferings, publish them in the hope that public opinion would be aroused, and plan to help those who had been imprisoned or impoverished to re-establish their lives.

After the declaration of war by the king of England, New Jersey passed a draft act, and Pennsylvania passed an act establishing a militia. There would be plenty for the new Meeting for Sufferings to do.

John Woolman experienced an impulsive and personal kind of satisfaction from these sessions. He had made a right decision in giving up his shop. He was more right with God than he had been before. He was able to give more time and clearer thought to these grave matters, when he had fewer worldly problems on his mind. He was less encumbered—freer!

He told Sarah about his new feeling of freedom as they rode home from Yearly Meeting.

He and Sarah often stopped at the old Woolman house in

Rancocas on their way back from a trip to Burlington. Elizabeth Woolman was growing older, and John liked to keep an eye on her. She had been able to accept her husband's death stalwartly. Asher was still at home with her, still a bachelor, farming the lands, tending the fruit trees and stock. The two youngest boys were away as apprentices, and her youngest daughter, Rachel, was now twenty-one, the only girl still unmarried.

The aging woman's face always lighted up when John, her most extraordinary son, paid her a visit. He was hardly her son any more; he had become her guardian and minister, and a guardian and father to her youngest children.

She took the face of her grandchild, Mary Woolman, between her hands and looked first down and then up at Sarah, smiling and nodding wordless approval of this well-raised child.

"Children grow richly on love and gentleness," she observed.

John Woolman brought a kind of glow with him whenever he stepped over the threshold into a home, whether it was his own door or someone else's. He moved in an increasing happiness and an increasing purpose as his spiritual powers improved and he expended them for others, and at the same time developed an immunity to the worldliness of his times. He watched with genuine joy as a multitude of other Friends shared his immunity, held to the full spirit of their faith, refused to participate in the struggle for power, refused to yield in their difference with the governor and Proprietors.

Those in the Assembly had gone as far as their consciences would permit. They had even voted large sums for "the King's use." But the actual declaration of war by England left them no alternative but to withdraw from the Assembly altogether. When the fall elections of 1756 rolled around, they gave up their seats, resigning or declining re-election, and asked their friends not to choose them in the coming election. Four Quakers were elected against their wishes, and they refused to take office. There had been twenty-eight Quakers in the Assembly of thirty-six, and after the momentous election of that year no more than a dozen remained. Since that time Friends have been cautious of holding public office.

They turned their attentions instead to an idea that had come to life among them at about the same time as their Meeting for Sufferings, and they founded the Friendly Association for Regaining and Preserving Peace with the Indians by Pacific Measures. Anthony Benezet was among its most active advocates and workers.

John Woolman was a party in spirit and fact to all of these happenings. None of them was the result of the thinking of one man or one mind, nor even the product of one man's courage. They came out of that deep unity within the Society of Friends, that unity which Friends constantly courted in their Meetings for Worship, for the Meeting for Worship was the starting point, the nourishing root, of all they believed and all they did.

A rare few ministers like John Woolman had the capacity to explore in spiritual planes farther than his contemporaries, and when he rose to speak on First Day mornings they unconsciously inclined their heads toward him to catch the total message. There were those John Woolman reached with his pen in his letters and essays whom he could not reach in person, and in that same memorable year of 1756 he began his *Journal*.

John Woolman's *Journal* is a thing of rare literary beauty. With its unadorned language, the deep humility of its tone, the gradual unfolding of its author's inner character, it has come down to us through almost two hundred years as a warm and living document. To his *Journal* Woolman committed an appraisal of himself and his development, from his childhood dreams, youthful errors, and conflicts, to the very close of his life, so that others might be guided by his testimony to unfailing, always available, divine guidance. Its sentences were laid down painstakingly and slowly upon rough rag paper with a quill pen, faint pencil lines drawn to keep his handwriting from its uphill tendencies. Woolman conscientiously omitted from it all sentiment, all reference to the worldlier side of his life, because these are not the things upon which the properly directed Christian mind dwells. Aided by the unsteady, wavering light of a candle, late at night or early in the morning (those times when he felt closest to God), John Woolman covered page after page with his scholarly language.

In these hours of retirement, too, he directed his love toward those in need of it. Since he had an unlimited source upon which to draw to replenish himself, he could spend himself generously on others. Letters came from his pen, letters of comfort and courage and reassurance, epistles of pure love, in which he shared the depths of himself with his fellow men.

"In this thy late affliction," a letter to a sick friend once said, "I've found deep fellow-feeling with thee. . . . A love clothes my mind while I write which is superior to all expression. . . ."

14

TIIE SOUTIILAND ONCE MORE

Love did not clothe every mind. In Massachusetts the captain of the militia was beating his drum in the public squares because the Massachusetts General Court had authorized the raising of 3500 volunteers. The governor of Connecticut reported that his colonists were "warmed with zeal for His Majesty's service." Pennsylvania, Virginia, Maryland, and North Carolina began plans to raise 5000 men.

At that point the French seemed to have every advantage in North America, and the British Crown seemed to be giving most of its attention to the war on the European continent. Montcalm, who was in charge of forces in Canada, marched down with his French and Indian troops to Lake George and captured Fort William Henry. Alarmed for fear the French would come all the way to Albany, the legislatures of both New York and Massachusetts were called into session to provide additional supplies and money. By that time the French had forts all the way from Duquesne to Canada.

But a change occurred in the British government that meant a change in the war picture in North America. William Pitt was made secretary of state at the end of 1756, and he turned his attention to North America where the French were making such progress. He planned to attack the French at three vital points: at Fort Duquesne in the Ohio Valley, at Fort Ticonderoga on Lake George in New York, and at the great fort of Quebec on the mouth of the St. Lawrence River. Breaking the power of the French in America could not be accomplished overnight; it might take years.

The Friends realized this as well as anyone else, and with saddened hearts they prepared themselves to face whatever hostility or hardship must be faced as a result of their beliefs.

The disordered world disturbed John Woolman waking and sleeping. More and more he needed to turn to prayer and reading of prayerful material; more and more he needed that moment before sleeping when he made his last conscious communication with God, or those happy intervals during the night when he would awaken to a sudden awareness of spiritual presence in the stillness and dark.

Those nights when he actually experienced a significant dream were particularly precious. They didn't happen often, but for him they were profoundly significant, truly visionary and message-laden.

With all the burdens of his people—war, slavery, taxation, conscription, politics—on his heart, John Woolman fell asleep one night at the home of a Friend in Burlington. After sleeping a short while he awoke. The moon had not yet risen, and his room and the world outside his window were pitch dark. As Woolman opened his eyes and watched, he saw five or six feet from his bed a light "about nine inches diameter." It was bright, most radiant at the center; yet he could look straight at it.

"As I lay still without any surprise looking upon it, words were spoken to my inward ear which filled my whole inward man . . . the words were *Certain Evidence of Divine Truth*, and were again repeated exactly in the same manner, whereupon the light disappeared."

The vision was reassuring. For John Woolman it confirmed what he already knew to be true, that his life was particularly dedicated to follow a light, no matter where it might lead him.

He had no secrets from his fellow men, because he had no cunning, and he discussed his vision with his friend the next morning.

"I feel confident that I was awake at the time," he said.

"It matters not," came the answer. "God can invade the mind at any hour."

When he described the experience to Sarah, she, too, accepted the dream as highly significant.

"The ministry is thy great mission."

Life held a kind of gentle, persistent excitement and anticipation for John Woolman. It was a continuing adventure in service.

During the winter months he began to feel another definite sense of assignment: the Southland. Eleven years had elapsed since his first trip to the Southern colonies. Perhaps with his added experience, his greater maturity, his increased confidence and faith, he could revitalize the Quaker message for them.

As soon as the snow had disappeared and the trails through the forests were dry enough, he prepared to set out. He planned to make the journey alone, but unexpectedly his brother Uriah, by this time through with his apprenticeship and in business in Philadelphia, offered to go along.

"I can journey part of the way with thee," he said flatly. "Mine is a business trip."

John Woolman by then was thirty-seven, settled, serious, even a little portly in his figure; Uriah was eight years younger and rather worldly.

"Thou understandest," he rebuked the younger man, "that I am going on a religious mission. It will not be a time for seeking material gain."

Uriah became annoyed in his own right.

"A little material gain is proper!" he retorted.

When John Woolman sensed the tension between himself and his brother, he paused, then replied in a gentle and loving tone, "Of course, thou mayst travel with me. I will ask the elders to give thee a certificate."

Uriah responded in a friendly tone, "My certificate can be worded suitably, and I shall go only part of the way with thee."

The two brothers mounted their horses a few days later and started out from Philadelphia, riding side by side as long as the trail would permit, single file when it grew narrow. Whenever John lapsed into a long period of silence, Uriah respected his withdrawal. He understood how deeply his brother was disturbed by this return into unpleasant memories, how deeply grieved he would be by what he was certain to find in provinces where too much wealth was created out of too much want and slavery.

One of John Woolman's pockets was heavier than the others, because it was full of silver coins. The Quaker custom of extending free hospitality to visiting Friends meant that he would be under some obligation to his hosts throughout the Southern journey. He had decided that he would rather pay with money from his own pocket than be obligated for his comforts to anyone deriving those comforts from the services of exploited human beings.

They traveled southward to Nottingham, almost at the Maryland border, and stayed overnight with John Churchman, Then they crossed into Maryland, and over the Susquehanna River.

Deeper and deeper into the economy that made Woolman so unhappy! They visited meetings when there were any and conducted meetings in private homes whenever the opportunity presented itself. Down through Maryland, across the Potomac and Rappahannock rivers into Virginia.

Whenever Woolman left a wealthy home he would turn and slip a hand into his pocket, producing some silver coins.

"May I speak with thee privately," he sometimes said to his host, and then would insist upon leaving money for the Negroes who had waited upon him. Or, if his host seemed like the kind who would object, Woolman would hand the money to the Negroes himself.

Woolman spoke with his whole personality, with his total life. He spoke to the consciences of slaveowners with words and with deeds. When profit was all they could understand, he spoke to them with cash.

And he addressed himself to the condition of any who opened a conversation with him. On the way he fell into company with a colonel of the militia, and John Woolman chose to discuss the subject closest to his heart.

"There is a great difference between people who labor moderately for their living, training up their children in frugality and business, and those who live on the labor of slaves," he observed, as an opener.

"Yes," replied the colonel, "but have you noticed how slothful the Negroes are and how many of them it takes to do one man's work in a day?"

"Free men," replied Woolman, "whose minds are properly on their business, find a satisfaction in the improving, cultivating, and providing for their families; but Negroes, laboring to support those who claim them as their property, expecting nothing but slavery during life, have not the like inducement to be industrious."

After a few moments of silence, Woolman added one more remark, "I believe that liberty is the natural right of all men equally."

The righteous exercise within John Woolman grew more intense as he passed plantation after plantation and saw the tragic contrasts between the slave huts and the white mansions, the dirt and rags and long hours of toiling without recompense in the sun by the slaves and the comforts and rich dress and ease of the owners. Tobacco-growing Maryland and Virginia were building their wealth on a foundation of poverty and misery. Tobacco itself was a habit-forming drug, Woolman reasoned. Only unhappiness could come of it.

His next conversation was with a civilian, a local landowner, who said, "Negroes are the offspring of Cain, their blackness being the mark of God set upon him after he murdered Abel, his brother."

John Woolman knew his Bible better than that, and he answered, "Noah and his family were all who survived the Flood according to Scripture; and as Noah was of Seth's race, the family of Cain was wholly destroyed."

He heard many more arguments and defenses for slavery, but John Woolman was a scholar as well as a minister. His replies came calmly and easily.

Woolman was not wandering along a random route. He had a definite direction as well as a definite purpose in mind. He was headed for Virginia Yearly Meeting, and he was counting off the days to make certain that he would arrive in Isle of Wight County in time for it. There he intended to speak to the leadership, the cream, of Southern Quakerdom. He felt a special conviction that Virginia Yearly Meeting was the place where his message would be most needed and would do the most good, for the decisions of a Yearly Meeting affected all of its member meetings.

He and Uriah reached Camp Creek Monthly Meeting the middle of May, then, since there was sufficient time, turned their horses' heads westward and traveled up the James River to reach those living in out-of-the-way places.

In war-minded Virginia, where so many were rushing into the militia, John Woolman met a young Friend who had been imprisoned for a while because he had refused to serve in the armed forces. The minister and the young man clasped hands and drew strength from each other. One such person could renew Woolman's hope for all of the Friends in the South.

And there were more! Another time he found a Friend who had no slaves and was laboring to support himself.

Woolman seemed to grow in stature as he continued on this, his second mission to the South, and his eloquence increased as he spoke in meeting after meeting, reasoned with slaveowner after slaveowner. Wherever he lodged, he left a loving rebuke for the conditions which he saw with his own eyes: little or no care given to Negro marriages, the taking of children from their parents and the separating of husbands and wives when slaves were resold, the field overseer with the whip in his hand to drive these "slothful" people, their insufficient clothing, the nakedness of their children.

The fine gold of the Quaker faith wore a noticeable tarnish in the South. Southern Quakers were departing from the Truth, were succumbing through tongue-in-cheek reasoning to luxuries derived from the misery of others.

By the time he reached Burleigh, his eloquence seemed to reach a new height under pressure of his great concern. He and the Burleigh Friends sat a long time in silence until at length

John Woolman felt within himself that compelling urge to speak, that message that had at last come into the form of words. Rising slowly in place, pausing to make certain of the content of his message, he began to share his thoughts with the Meeting. That "powerful operation of Divine Love" within him, once shared, caught up everyone, and even the most resistant were forced to say that the Meeting at which John Woolman had spoken had been an edifying Meeting.

He and Uriah were on their way back down the James River by this time, stopping at Black Water, headed for Western Branch in Isle of Wight County.

In Virginia, where the Society of Friends did not begin to possess the strength that it had in Pennsylvania and New Jersey, a visit from a weighty Friend with a powerful gift of ministry was profoundly important to its members. Samuel Fothergill had come to them two years before, and here came the beloved John Woolman for a second time.

"A committee will report upon the Queries," was one of the first things they told him, and he was overjoyed.

They had appointed a committee to examine the Pennsylvania Queries with an eye to adopting them to their own use. The wild fleeting notion that perhaps Virginia would adopt a strong Query on slavery, as strong as Pennsylvania's, excited Woolman for a moment. His common sense dismissed it almost as quickly as it occurred to him. The whole level of the faith was lower here. "Mixed with the world in whose spirit they dwell," Fothergill had said of Maryland and Virginia.

Woolman was deeply sensitive to people, and he could judge very well the situation in Virginia. He must do all that he could; he must use every ounce of influence that he could muster; but he must not expect too much. He could only hope that in time the Light would reach their hearts.

He plunged into the work of the sessions and conferences, spoke gently but confidently, firmly but sympathetically.

"We are assembled to support the Truth," he cautioned the Virginia Friends. "It is necessary for us to dwell deep and act in that wisdom which is pure."

The words were a little oblique, but the Friends understood them, and they did "dwell deep" in the question of the Slavery Query.

But they were not ready to throw over their whole pattern of living. It was not so easy in the South as it was in Pennsylvania. They considered the Query: "Are there any concerned in the importation of Negroes, or buying them after imported?"

It was too strong. In order to achieve the complete unity of the group, the Meeting had to water it down to: "Are any concerned in the importation of Negroes or buying them to trade in?"

It was progress, John Woolman reminded himself, as he sat and listened to the proceedings. Southern Friends had gone a step farther in the right direction.

But when he heard them adopt a Query against buying or selling goods that had been captured at sea and unlawfully imported, he was on his feet, pointing out their inconsistency.

Did they not realize, he asked them, that buying any merchandise taken by the sword was against Friends' principles? They were objecting to prize goods, or war booty, captured at sea; yet Negroes were really captives of war. Negroes were taken by stealth and imported against their will. Since they were fellow human beings, that made the deed so much more evil.

Virginia Friends listened carefully and respectfully, but they made no further improvement in their Query on slavery;

and John Woolman had to realize that he had accomplished as much as he could for the moment. He must be patient and pray for future progress.

Friends were grateful for his visit in any event, and those who agreed with his views on slavery were frankly so.

"The Meeting was attended with the company of our worthy Friend John Woolman," said the minutes, "from the Province of New Jersey, being on a religious visit to us who produced his certificate from the Monthly Meeting at Burlington dated the 2nd day 5th month, 1757. He was accompanied by his brother Uriah Woolman, a private Friend. . . ."

Virginia was not the end of his journey. John Woolman set out for North Carolina to visit Wells Creek Monthly Meeting (Perquimans), and from there to go on to New Garden. At New Garden Uriah turned homeward, but John went on to Simons Creek (Pasquotank) and to Newbegun Creek.

At length he turned homeward, still visiting Friends' homes and meetings as he traveled, back into Virginia, working his way northward.

Approaching the end of his journey, John Woolman lay on his back on the ground one night looking straight up into the stars that shone between the branches of the trees. In spite of the mosquitoes buzzing around him and the dampness of the ground under him, it was a good time to reflect.

He had been traveling full two months and would have covered over eleven hundred miles of wilderness. The journey had been most fruitful. Even though he had seen much to discourage him, he knew he had won some hearts, disturbed some consciences with the Truth, and encouraged many more who were standing alone.

The hoot of a night owl broke in upon his thoughts, but the liquid contralto tone flowed into his meditations. Every creature that spoke, spoke of creation.

Woolman stretched his tired limbs, feeling suddenly a deep
sense of satisfaction with this, his second Southern journey. It
had really been more successful than the first. He must be
patient with people, infinitely patient. Their thinking could
be raised to a new level in time.

He hoped he had executed his mission to his fullest ability.
The ministry was the rarest duty to which a man could be
called. What would be his next assignment, he pondered as
he closed his eyes.

15

THE QUARTERING OF SOLDIERS

"The calamities of war were now increasing," John Woolman confided to his *Journal* after his return from his second Southern journey. "The frontier inhabitants of Pennsylvania were frequently surprised; some slain, and many taken captive by the Indians."

The French and Indian War that had started two years earlier was spreading over colonial America until it was the prime topic of the day. The home government in England, led by Pitt, was paying more and more attention to the colonial phase of the war known in Europe as the Seven Years' War, sending troops from Great Britain as well as enlisting colonials, promising to provide arms and ammunition and reimburse the provincial governments for clothing and salaries of colonial soldiers. Young men were responding through the South, New York, and New England, and the war fever was catching on in New Jersey and Pennsylvania, although not at the same breath-taking rate of speed.

John Woolman returned home to find troops drilling in Mount Holly. Seeing them go through their maneuvers on an open green recalled his dream: the streams of red that he had seen in the sky, the men in "military posture," all improving in the discipline of war.

He turned his back on the drilling troops and walked homeward, stepping over the threshold into an atmosphere of love and understanding. His daughter was seven; his son would never be tempted into military service. Sarah sat with her head bent over her needlework, and he eased his large frame into a chair near her. Sensing his burden, she acknowledged his presence with a faint inclination of her head and waited until he was ready to speak.

"I have had fresh opportunity to see and consider the advantage of living in the real substance of religion," he said at last, "where practice doth harmonize with principle."

She had seen what her husband had seen: young men of the Society having to decide between loyalty to their country and loyalty to their Society. Some were taking up arms, others were risking freedom and property to ignore the military appeal, still others left their homes and "tarried abroad" until it was over. Man was a complex creature, they both knew. Many Friends taking up arms were upright-hearted; many who refused to fight were less so in other ways.

"Where men profess to be so meek and heavenly minded, and to have their trust so firmly settled in God that they cannot join in wars, and yet by their spirit and conduct in common life manifest a contrary disposition, their difficulties are great at such a time."

He was referring to slavekeepers. Sarah realized that he was thinking out loud, trying to find his own way among the minds of men. He was remembering what he had just seen in the Southland.

"Thou needest to talk with Anthony Benezet and Israel Pemberton," Sarah suggested.

They were always good for him.

"The Friendly Association has been meeting almost every month while thou wast away," she added. "It has considered many grievances of the Indians. It has raised funds among the Friends to buy gifts of clothing, blankets, and silver medals for the Indians; it has been urging the governor to arrange another conference with the Senecas and Delawares; in Seventh Month it sent an address to the Pennsylvania Assembly."

Woolman had been on his way home from Carolina in July.

"Dost thou know the content of the address?"

"Yes, I think so. It reminded the Assembly that many peaceful conferences had been held with the Indians and that just grounds for making peace with them could be found. It offered the services of the Friends in bringing about an alliance with the Indians as proof of the loyalty of the Friends to the king and even offered to advance the necessary funds."

Friends Benezet and Pemberton were leading figures in the Friendly Association for Gaining and Preserving Peace with the Indians by Pacific Measures, and they were both bound to be at Yearly Meeting.

He and Benezet and Pemberton came together in many ways when they all reached Philadelphia. They met in sessions of the Meeting for Sufferings, in general sessions, and on the committee designated to write the annual epistle to to London Yearly Meeting.

"Some Friends in diverse parts of these provinces have been subjected to sufferings for not complying with the injunctions of the laws passed for military services and preparations," the epistle reported to the parent meeting.

After every Yearly Meeting personal letters were exchanged across the ocean; and since Samuel Fothergill had returned to London after his long visit in America, many American Friends wrote him letters about the Yearly Meeting of 1757.

"There continues to be a great shaking amongst our dry bones," Benezet told him. "The hearts of many amongst us, especially the youth, are touched with love and zeal for God. May they abide the trial better than I have done."

John Churchman felt a deep hope out of that Yearly Meeting, for he wrote to Fothergill: "I think that this Yearly Meeting was as much favoured as any meeting I was ever in; which is, indeed, great cause of solemn thankfulness. We had the company of many of our youth, who sat with a reverent attention, and some spoke to the business to my admiration."

They were all encouraged by Yearly Meeting, sensing a deep strength in the Society.

But the winter following that Yearly Meeting saw the intensification of the war fever. The year 1758 was the one in which the crown was gathering its strength to drive the French out of North America. In April of that year the privacy of John Woolman's very home was invaded. An officer and two men, swords clanking, voices loud and brash from their military training, arrived at his door.

"Two soldiers will be quartered in your home," they told him. "You will of course be reimbursed, six shillings per week per man."

Other soldiers were being quartered on Woolman's neighbors, but the experience came as a shock. Woolman was not prepared to give answer. He stood for a moment in silence, trying to reconcile his Christian principles with receiving pay for entertaining soldiers. It was all legal enough. After some reflection he replied to the men:

"I cannot refuse hospitality to a fellow man, and so I shall admit the soldiers to my home, but I cannot do so for hire."

The officer sneered, "I think you might do so and be consistent with your religious principles."

Woolman made no reply. As soon as his visitors had disappeared, he strode out of the house and out into the orchards alone. His heart and mind had been thrown into a sudden confusion of fear and doubt. He walked rapidly across the field trying to recover his composure. These gruff, ill-bred, careless-minded men were going to destroy the sweet peace of his life. Now, in the spring, when his orchards and lands demanded so much of his time away from the house, they would be with his wife and daughter. The short grass brushed against his shoes as he walked, until he came to a large rock and sat down. There in the mild breeze that stirred his hair he could pause and pray for strength and protection. He sat a long time, until the sudden outburst of excitement within him died down and his equilibrium returned. Then he walked slowly back to the house.

He found Sarah calmly carrying linens to prepare the beds for the expected guests. Beloved wife! Her faith was more steadfast than his.

Only one soldier arrived. The Woolmans received him as a brother, gave him every comfort their house could offer, shared their board with him, and accepted his presence with confidence and trust, responding with gentleness to his every roughness.

Day by day they watched their visitor lose his arrogance and his noisiness, speak more softly, walk more lightly in his heavy boots, find little favors to do for Mary, even carry water or wood for Sarah. He remained rather shy of John Woolman —the man who was as big and strong as himself and yet who, he knew, would do him no violence no matter what his own behavior might be. It would have embarrassed him, he admitted, to strike a man who would not strike back.

"He tarried at my house about two weeks and behaved himself civilly," Woolman said in his *Journal*.

When John Woolman was riding on horseback across his fields one day, he saw the officer waiting near the house for him, and at first he thought that this would be the billeting of another soldier.

"I have come to pay you for the soldier who stayed with you," the officer explained.

"I cannot accept pay," Woolman reminded him. "I admitted the man into my house in a passive obedience to authority."

Something within even this hard-shelled man was touched by Woolman's spirit, and as Woolman turned his horse's head away the officer said, "I am obliged to you."

Disturbed lest the officer not fully understand his motives, John Woolman sought him out a few days later and explained to him at length why he had refused to accept pay for the soldier's keep.

16

"IT IS NOT A TIME FOR DELAY"

Some of John Woolman's deepest meditation and most careful thinking went into his pen. Out of his candlelit hours and his First Day afternoons had come his essay on the keeping of Negroes, and more essays were accumulating on his writing table. The essays were as much a part of John Woolman's soul as his *Journal*; for they were the fruit of his hours alone with God, when thinking was the purest, undisturbed by creaturely considerations. Composed painstakingly between *Journal* entries and letters, the essays would someday be collected under the modest title, *Serious Considerations on Various Subjects of Importance*. One of them, "On Pure Wisdom and Human Policy," belongs to this period of his life when he was so torn by the problems of war and slavery.

"To have our Trust settled in the Lord, and not to seek after, nor desire outward treasures," it began. "Pure Wisdom leads people into lowliness of mind, in which they learn resignation to the Divine Will . . . While we proceed in this precious way . . ."

Woolman wrote on and on in his own precious and exquisite prose, having no idea that he was one of America's earliest literary figures.

He delved into the writings of other religious men, as books came to America from Europe. He cared not what a man's denomination was if he was a true saint. When he read *Imitation of Christ* by Thomas à Kempis, he was so moved by it that he made an entry in his *Journal:*

"I have been informed that Thomas à Kempis lived and died in the profession of the Roman Catholic religion; and, in reading his writings, I have believed him to be a man of a true Christian spirit, as fully so as many who died martyrs because they could not join with some superstitions in that church. All true Christians are of the same spirit, but their gifts are diverse."

These spiritual retreats gave John Woolman strength as the tides of history rolled up around him.

The French and Indians still had the better of the war in America. The British launched the first of their major campaigns against the French at Crown Point on Lake George in July. They marched their troops up the western shore of the lake, and Indian scouts warned Montcalm that they were coming. Montcalm knew the wilderness; the British did not; and Montcalm moved south from Crown Point and met the enemy at Ticonderoga. There, with a much smaller force, he visited another defeat upon the British.

The battle of Ticonderoga made gloomy news for the English colonies. The drums beat louder than ever in the public squares, calling men to serve in the armed forces. The Friends persisted in their efforts to negotiate with the Indians and prodded both Indians and the Pennsylvania government into holding several conferences at Easton and Lancaster. The Pennsylvania government allowed itself to be prodded, since its Assembly still opposed the raising of large numbers of troops. The troops were coming from other colonies: nearly twenty thousand from parts north of Pennsylvania had been raised for the Crown Point campaign; some five thousand from the Southern colonies for the forthcoming campaign against Fort Duquesne.

The British navy, far superior to the French, was patrolling the seas between Europe and America, and a great fleet trimmed sail at Halifax, bringing huge land troops and naval forces to attack Louisbourg and Quebec. Louisbourg, on the southern coast of the Island of Newfoundland, guarded the entrance to the St. Lawrence River, and it was a French stronghold.

The English fleet of twenty-two ships and fifteen frigates sailed from Halifax to Louisbourg, and after waiting for the surf to die down troops went ashore under protection of the ships' guns. They fought their way through defenses of felled trees and branches, and in one day conquered the fort. James Wolfe was a brigade commander in that attack, and he acquitted himself with such skill and valor that he was made a major general for the attack on Quebec.

First the rumors flew, then letters traveling with the mounted postman carried news of the victory down over the post roads, then news items in the papers, telling that the war had taken a favorable turn for the English.

John Woolman was visiting at the Quarterly Meeting in Chester County and at other meetings in Philadelphia County when these rumors of a British naval and land victory were spreading. The news did not send his pulse up or strike him with sudden excitement. As he visited Meetings for Worship or sat beside sickbeds, he tried to dismiss it from his mind; but the mixed feelings among Friends about military service and the payment of war taxes were stirred into new debate by every major military event. On this short trip Woolman was approached by a Friend about the payment of the war tax.

"I wanted an opportunity to talk to someone who shared my scruple," said Woolman's visitor.

Woolman conversed with him in gentle tones for some time, and at last the man concluded, "We must suffer distraint of goods rather than pay actively toward supporting the war."

Those who consulted Woolman usually went away with more courage than they brought to the interview.

Woolman did not return to Mount Holly until he had attended the Monthly Meeting in Philadelphia, and there he found the group exercised because some of its members had bought Negro slaves. Since this was not his own Monthly Meeting he sat quietly while others spoke, feeling a secret thrill as the sense of the Meeting concluded that the minute on slavery must be sent on to Quarterly Meeting.

He was not back in Mount Holly long when news reached him that the Quarterly Meeting had concluded to raise the question of slavery at the impending Yearly Meeting. He hurried to Sarah with the open letter in his hand.

"Perhaps this year we shall be able to strengthen the Query on slavery!"

"It has grown stronger every time they have considered it," she reminded him.

Mixed with his excitement was a sudden feeling of his limited ability. What was his own weight, he wondered, amongst the more than a thousand Friends who would assemble at Burlington? He could not plan his words, nor even his thoughts in advance, for that would not be the Quaker way. He and they must assemble in worship and, united with one another and with God, hope that a clear message could reach the Meeting through one or more of them. Anthony Benezet would be there, and so would many others who thought as he did. But with them would be those who resisted, who had even turned cool in their attitude toward such extremists as himself.

He must court no man's hostility; he must arouse none to anger; he must remember that nothing could be accomplished at Yearly Meeting except through love. He must retire and prepare his own heart for this grave experience. With as much humility as the small boy who had once sat in the grass spelling his way through the Scripture searching for an answer to a strange dream, John Woolman sat down with his Bible once more. "Settle it therefore in your minds, not to meditate beforehand how to answer; for I will give you the mouth and wisdom, which none of your adversaries will be able to withstand or contradict," was the advice he knew he would find.

Constantly through his memory flashed the kaleidoscope of all he had seen in the Southland and even near at hand; the bills of sale he had written and those he had refused to write; the wills he had drawn when he had persuaded owners to liberate their slaves; the persons with whom he had reasoned successfully about slavekeeping. He had been given the mouth and wisdom on these occasions. Would he could be granted them again!

A continuous prayer coursed through his mind as he packed saddlebags, as he and Sarah mounted, as they rode along, as they approached Burlington. When he and his wife and child arrived at the home of the Friends in Burlington who would be their hosts for the week of conferences, his prayers flowed on as he unsaddled his horses, conversed politely, or ate. When he retired he drew his whole being together into the concentration in which so many years of practice had made him skillful.

If he could be given the mouth and wisdom . . .

Slavery was only one of many important matters drawing Friends together in that momentous year, and so the gathering was large. John Woolman entered the meeting hall and sat down in the silent worship that opened the first session and dutifully surrendered himself up to it. As the Meeting moved into discussion he tried to overcome his preoccupation with slavery and contribute what he could to other questions, but he found it almost impossible to shake off the burden of slavery from his mind.

"During the several sittings of the said Meeting, my mind was frequently covered with inward prayer, and I could say with David, 'that tears were my meat day and night.' The case of slave-keeping lay heavy upon me, nor did I find any engagement to speak directly to any other matter before the Meeting."

When the subject that troubled Woolman was at last opened, he still did not speak immediately. He sat in the gathering tension, as the interest of the Meeting deepened into suspense, and listened to other weighty Quakers expressing their views.

He looked at the faces of those who spoke. They were deeply in earnest, profoundly disturbed. None actually spoke openly in favor of the practice of slavekeeping. They were simply thinking out loud, striving for an answer, laboring together for a solution.

At the writing table up front sat the learned Israel Pemberton, recording clerk, one of the most prominent importing and exporting merchants of Philadelphia. For the past twenty years he had been a courageous spokesman for Quaker principles in Pennsylvania affairs. Even with all the pressures that his business crowded upon him, he always had time to serve others. He was one of the founders and manager, until he died, of the Philadelphia Hospital; he was clerk for the Quaker schools; and he was a leader in the founding of the Friendly Association and recording clerk for Philadelphia Yearly Meeting for fifteen years.

There were many like Israel Pemberton in that Yearly Meeting, and they all sat immersed in thought, part of the striving. When several had spoken, the trend began to develop that Yearly Meeting ought to wait still longer. Perhaps in a later year a way would be found. The uneasiness began to dissolve a little as those who owned slaves yearned toward the delay. If Friends patiently continued under the exercise, the Lord in time to come might open a way for the deliverance of these people.

The ache in Woolman's heart became so intense that he thought it would break. He delved deeper into prayer until every fiber of his being reached a trembling tensity. The tears that were his "meat night and day" gathered in his eyes as his hands fumbled toward the back of the bench in front of him. Within him was gathering the nebula of his message, coming together, taking shape, becoming words, assuming possession of him, driving him to his feet, compelling him to speak.

Quaking, yet confident, John Woolman began to talk, calling upon all of his years of experience as a minister.

"My mind is often led to consider the purity of the Divine Being, and the justice of His judgments; and herein my soul is covered with awfulness. I cannot omit to hint of some cases where people have not been treated with the purity of justice, and the event hath been lamentable. Many slaves on this continent are oppressed, and their cries have reached the ears of the Most High. Such are the purity and certainty of His judgments, that He cannot be partial in our favour. In infinite love and goodness He hath opened our understanding from time to time respecting our duty toward this people."

John Woolman's strong voice, enriched by the inspiration that it felt, vibrated through the great room.

"It is not a time for delay. Should we now be sensible of what He requires of us, and through a respect to the private interest of some persons, or through a regard to some friendships which do not stand on the immutable foundation, neglect to do our duty in firmness and constancy, still waiting for some extraordinary means to bring about their freedom, God may by terrible things in righteousness answer us in this matter."

He had spoken to everyone's condition. The Meeting sat silently united, like a set of fine lenses at last brought into perfect focus. The presiding clerk knew the sense of the gathering and waited with the rest as Israel Pemberton's quill moved over the paper. The Meeting was writing this minute.

"After weighty consideration of the circumstances of Friends within the compass of this Meeting, who have any Negro or other slaves, . . . there appears to be a unanimous concern prevailing to put a stop to the increase of the practice of importing, buying, selling, or keeping slaves for term of life; or purchasing them for such a number of years, as manifests that such purchasers do only in terms, and not in fact, avoid the imputation of being keepers of slaves."

17

THE SPRING OF LIVING MINISTRY

The Friends had passed through an hour of great decision, and once the path they were to travel had been lighted they pursued it with faith and enthusiasm. Many in the Yearly Meeting, whose thinking had been unresolved before the sessions opened, asked frankly that a rule be made to punish Friends in the future who might be guilty of buying slaves.

The way was clear to them for the next hundred years. They were destined to lead the fight for emancipation from then on, to risk loss of life and property in operating the underground railroad during the pre-Civil War years, to shield runaways, to rescue the abused and nurse the injured. The whole movement that had begun with a voiced disaffection in a small Germantown Meeting in 1688 came to fruition in Burlington in 1758 and ultimately became the great abolitionist crusade.

And the personality of John Woolman—single-minded saint—was the focal point at which the diverse rays of thinking came together and then radiated out over America.

With his great joy, tempered by humility, he plunged into the rest of the program that developed out of the Yearly Meeting. He, John Scarborough, John Churchman, John Sykes, and Daniel Stanton were approved by the Meeting to undertake a special service: to visit and treat with all such Friends who had any slaves.

"Proceed in the wisdom of Truth," the Meeting advised its special committee.

"And if after the sense and judgment of this Meeting, now given against every branch of this practice, any professing with us should persist to vindicate it, and be concerned in importing, selling, or purchasing slaves, the respective Monthly Meetings to which they belong should manifest their disunion with such persons, by refusing to permit them to sit in Meetings for discipline, or to be employed in the affairs of Truth, or to receive from them any contribution towards the relief of the poor, or other services of the Meeting," Israel Pemberton added to the minute.

Conclusive and final, that minute meant ultimate banishment from membership in the Society for all of those who, within a reasonable length of time, did not divest themselves of their slaves by liberating them and then forever after refrain from being a party to the evil institution.

Before Yearly Meeting could adjourn, the epistles to other Yearly Meetings and to the Quarterly and Monthly Meetings under the jurisdiction of the Philadelphia Yearly Meeting had to be composed.

John Churchman and Israel Pemberton wrote the London epistle, and for their Friends abroad they described the results as follows:

"Our Meeting hath been large and the spring of living ministry freely opened therein. . . ."

John Woolman and Samuel Smith sat down together to write the epistle to North Carolina.

Gathering about them the services of many more, the Friends designated to treat with slaveholders began their visitations immediately after Yearly Meeting. The Eleventh Month found John Woolman traveling toward Concord in southeastern Pennsylvania. In Concord Quarterly Meeting he met with many loved Friends from both Pennsylvania and England and found them still animated and stimulated by the Yearly Meeting just passed. And there were young people there who were eager to know him.

"It was a precious, reviving opportunity," he said.

He called at the homes of Friends who owned slaves, as his Yearly Meeting had instructed him to do, and reasoned with them lovingly. He visited the sick while he was about it. From Concord he pushed on westward to the Quarterly Meeting at London Grove.

From one of these meetings he and several other Friends went home with Thomas Woodward to have dinner and perhaps to spend the night. Thomas Woodward was a weighty Friend in his community, a well-to-do farmer whose avocation was bookbinding. A Negro opened the door to them when they approached the house, and other Negroes moved about to wait upon them as they walked into the great living room. John Woolman turned to his host and asked the penetrating question:

"Are these Negroes slaves or are they paid servants?"

Thomas Woodward had to admit that they were slaves.

Without a comment of any kind, John Woolman walked out of the house. Thomas Woodward knew how he felt; he knew what had occurred at Yearly Meeting. Thomas Woodward was a learned man who did not need to be treated with in one-syllable words.

Woolman's estimate of Woodward's personality was entirely accurate, because the sensitive Woodward did not sleep well that night, and the next morning he announced to his wife and remaining guests:

"I must manumit my slaves."

The announcement startled everyone.

"I cannot keep slaves in my home if they are going to cost me the friendship of such men as John Woolman," was his flat conclusion.

Not only did Thomas Woodward free his slaves; he joined the committee making visitations upon others who still held slaves.

John Woolman meanwhile was finding that Quarterly Meetings were spending long hours on the issue of the war, and where questions of serving in the armed forces or paying war taxes were concerned the Meetings were far from united. They expressed their disunity by endless and (so John Woolman thought) pointless debate.

After sitting through several sessions that lasted from five to eight hours, John Woolman found his patience tried to the breaking point, and he made the terse entry in his *Journal:*

"It behooves all to be cautious how they detain a meeting, especially when they have sat six or seven hours, and have a good way to ride home. In 300 minutes are 5 hours, and he that improperly detains three hundred people one minute in a meeting, besides other evils that attend it, does an injury like that of imprisoning one man 5 hours without cause. After this meeting I rode home."

He rode home to his farmland and orchards to set things to rights so that he could resume his travels. He must make every effort, he realized, to be patient with those who suffered from indecision. Indecision had haunted his own younger years; he had tasted its embarrassment deeply.

Some of this indecision on war issues was certainly coming out of the war news itself. After the British victory at Louisbourg, reports came of another victory at Fort Duquesne, and that touched much more closely upon the lives of Pennsylvanians. The fort that had once so ignominiously fallen to the French under the stupid command of Braddock was finally retaken. Approaching the fort over the same route that had already been cut through the wilderness by Braddock, a force of nearly three thousand men under George Washington of Virginia and Colonel Armstrong of Pennsylvania made the attack. The French had been overconfident and had withdrawn some of their troops, and when the vastly superior British forces approached, they blew up their magazine and withdrew. Under the clouds of smoke rising into the sky from the exploding ammunition supplies, the British advanced upon the fort and occupied it.

They renamed the French stronghold Pittsburgh in honor of William Pitt, whose genius was directing a series of victories all over the world.

Pitt exhorted the colonies to further effort after the stimulation of the two great victories, and the colonies were responding with increased loyalty and devotion to the mother country. More young men responded to the mustering drum; more troops drilled and trained in the public squares; the powerful British navy continued to patrol the high seas.

Friends troubled by war taxes and the draft continued to debate their virtues and to suffer consequences when they resisted; Friends appointed to treat with slaveholders continued to go quietly about their appointed task.

Between the momentous Yearly Meeting of 1758 and the

next one, John Woolman traveled abroad whenever the demands of his lands would permit. He went out with John Sykes and Daniel Stanton in December. He spent a week in Philadelphia in January, where he and John Churchman did some visiting together. In March he was in Philadelphia again for the general Spring Meeting, and he and John Churchman visited slavekeepers in the city. In June he traveled down to Salem, spent seven days with South Jersey Friends, attending their First Day, Monthly, and Quarterly Meetings. Sometimes he was silent in worship; sometimes he spoke with great eloquence and warmth.

Slavery was the heavy burden on his mind, and he could only relieve that burden by speaking of it. July found him traveling from house to house alone, pleading, reasoning, sitting in silent communion.

"Man is born to labour," he would point out. "But where the life of one is made grievous by the rigour of another, it entails misery on both."

His efforts and the efforts of others working with him paid off richly during the year, and by the next Yearly Meeting those laboring on slavery were gratified to see how the concern had spread and won new adherents during the year. Most of the epistles that went out from the 1759 Yearly Meeting recommended that Friends labor against buying and keeping slaves.

John Woolman was just as sensitive to people as he was to God. He knew when a listener responded favorably to his thinking and when the listener withdrew. He knew, too, that he could not be so forthright in his own thinking and speaking and ministering without having to pay the price in friendship of those whose consciences he embarrassed. Yet peace to John Woolman meant peace with everyone, and he reflected sorrowfully upon the number of Friends who had become shy of him because of his views on slavery.

One in particular worried Woolman, a Friend of affluence and weight in the Meeting. False pride did not exist within John Woolman, nor pride of any kind, and after he had considered the barrier between himself and the unfriendly Friend he called at the man's house and humbly asked admittance.

"I desire an opportunity to speak with thee alone."

The door opened wide, and Woolman and his host went into a room where they would not be overheard or interrupted and sat down together.

It wasn't easy to do. Woolman sat silently for a moment before he could speak, and at last he said:

"Thou art distant; thou hast withdrawn from me; and I came in the hope that we could search out to the bottom the causes of the unfriendly feeling between us."

It would have been an obtuse man indeed who could have resisted so loving an approach. They sat in conversation a long time, striving to be frank with each other, turning over and "searching out" one point after another, until their differences were resolved.

At long last, John Woolman arose to leave, clasping the hand of the man who a few hours before had held himself aloof. Now his host smiled graciously as he escorted him to the door, tarried there a moment longer in a few last words of conversation, and stood in the open doorway so that he could wave to John Woolman one last time as he disappeared down the road.

It was the inexhaustible spring of living ministry within John Woolman that supplied him and supplied everyone with whom he ever associated with the vitality they needed to hew to their beliefs. Bubbling quietly and constantly, deep in the peaceful green forest of his faith, it strengthened him for one responsibility after another, gave him the words to utter when words were needed, helped him to keep silent when silence was wisest, washed clean his thoughts and his vision, replenished his courage.

18

"MY APPETITE FAILED"

Military victories, the lust for power, and national pride flourished all around Woolman and the Society of Friends, but his ministry and the direction of the Society did not change.

The British Empire was coming into being, bursting into glory all over the world. During the few months after the Yearly Meeting of 1759 a series of victories on land and sea launched Great Britain on her brilliant career as a world power.

Ticonderoga had already been taken and Fort Niagara had been captured when General Wolfe, with a huge army supported by a large fleet, moved upon the rocky stronghold of Quebec that was under Montcalm's command. Wolfe tried to entice Montcalm down from his high perch, but to no avail. At last, under cover of night, Wolfe led his men up the precipitous sides to the Plains of Abraham outside of the town, and at daylight they were ready to meet the French. Both Montcalm and Wolfe were fatally wounded in the battle, but both lived long enough to know the outcome—defeat for the French, victory for the English.

The conquest of Quebec was the most important of all of Britain's victories as far as the colonists were concerned, because it meant the end of French power in the New World; and although the war in Europe dragged on until 1763, it really ended in America in 1759.

The debates and heart searchings about military conscription and war taxes could recede into the background for a little while. Quakerdom could relax a little—all except Mount Holly.

"In the winter of 1759, the smallpox being in our town, and many being inoculated, of which a few died, some things were opened in my mind," John Woolman noted.

The ever recurring, ever ugly, ever terrifying smallpox struck Mount Holly. Many were the treatments and attempted preventives, but everyone knew there was no cure. Most people caught it at some time in their lives; some recovered and knew they would never have it again; others, like Elizabeth Woolman, died horribly. Nearly a fourth of all the people who were born in the eighteenth century died of smallpox. Smallpox was no respecter of rank or prestige. Even the Friends, who placed so much emphasis on personal cleanliness and nourishing food, were stricken by it.

The medical profession had been experimenting with inoculations for many years, but its methods were still woefully crude. Sometimes the well person was brought to the bedside of the stricken, a small gash made in his arm, and a bit of the matter transferred to the gash. Another method was to prick the skin with a needle that had been dipped into a pox.

A third was to run a string through a pox and then bind the string up in the gash on the well person's arm.

John Woolman remembered his sister's death as the new epidemic swept over Mount Holly, and he wondered if he would have the strength to face the sight of his wife or daughter, or both, covered with the loathsome, disfiguring sores. He had to make a terrible decision: to permit them to be inoculated or not to permit them. Many died from the inoculation. This thing called smallpox, this blight, seemed to him like a messenger from the Almighty, and only increased personal virtue could prevent it, really. As a result, his decision was not to allow Sarah, Mary, or himself to be inoculated, and he clung to that decision all through the winter until the epidemic faded with the disappearing cold and the spring returned with its warm winds and out-of-door exercise once more. Luckily his family had not been touched.

The returning spring stirred John Woolman's blood as it did everyone else's.

"I feel a sympathy in my mind with Friends eastward," he said to Samuel Eastburn, another Friends' minister, who lived in Bucks County, Pennsylvania.

That was the beginning of another New England journey.

After his partial success at Virginia Yearly Meeting, and his overwhelming success at Philadelphia Yearly Meeting, John Woolman could not rest until he had carried his slavery message to New England, the second largest Yearly Meeting in America. So he and Samuel Eastburn set out together on April 17, 1760.

It was harder than anyone realized for a devoted father and husband to absent himself from his family, but when conscience dictated that John Woolman take up a mission he must obey no matter how deeply he yearned for the com-

panionship of his wife and daughter. Before starting, he
wrote several letters on local affairs in which he had a responsibility, and one to John Smith in which he could not help
hinting that he was worried about Sarah.

"Beloved Friend . . . I hope my dear wife will be noticed by her friends. . . ."

He and Samuel Eastburn traveled the familiar road across
Jersey, and on the way northward visited meetings at Wood-
bridge, Rahway, and Plainfield. They were in time for the
Monthly Meeting at Rahway. The meetings on Long Island
were next on their route, and there the need for help from
visiting ministers was great indeed. John Woolman found the
"spring of the ministry often low," and he struggled against
the temptation to linger at these local meetings too long. The
drive to reach New England Yearly Meeting kept him moving, though, and he rode as though Rhode Island were a
magnet and he a fragment of sensitive metal.

At Jericho, on Long Island, he wrote home to his wife:

"Dearly Beloved Wife, We are favoured with health; have been
at sundry meetings in East Jersey and on this island. My mind
hath been much in an inward, watchful frame since I left thee,
greatly desiring that our proceedings may be singly in the will of
our Heavenly Father. . . . Since I left you I have often an engaging love and affection towards thee and my daughter, and
friends about home, and going out at this time, when sickness is
so great amongst you, is a trial upon me. . . ."

He and Eastburn took a boat from the east end of Long
Island to New London and while they were out on Long Island Sound a sudden squall sent the waves crashing against
their small craft. It was only one of a multitude of dangers
which a traveler had to face in colonial times. They put ashore
safely and went on to Narragansett.

"Dost thou know Thomas Hazard?" Woolman asked his traveling companion eagerly.

Samuel Eastburn shook his head. He was looking forward to that experience.

The closer John Woolman came to Narragansett and Newport the more vividly he recalled Thomas Hazard and his stand against slavery. His other New England journey had been thirteen years earlier, but the years melted together. Woolman remembered the worldly, slavekeeping, slave-trading communities.

But between his first and second journeys a vast change had taken place in Woolman. The individual possessed of an individual's righteousness had been replaced by a fully developed minister who came as the voice of the largest Yearly Meeting in America.

The Meetings felt the impact of a greater Woolman, a man grown richer in his mystical and oratorical powers, stronger in his conviction and direction. Friends within the seclusion of their wealthy homes were disturbed by his clear thinking, his penetrating gentleness, as he called upon them and endeavored to restore some of the quality of mercy to their hearts.

Sparing themselves not at all, Woolman and Eastburn labored from one Meeting to another on the mainland around Narragansett Bay, and from one home to another. John Woolman looked upon all that he saw with a dubious eye. Tensions and anxieties accumulated within him as he noted the increased amount of slavekeeping that went hand in hand with increased prosperity.

Five Meetings in Narragansett, then on to Newport on Rhode Island.

Newport, in spite of being inconveniently located out on an island, was the meeting place of the New England Yearly

Meeting. It was a wealthy town, a thriving seaport. Newport had been close to the pulse of the French and Indian War, and even in 1760, when the worst of the war was over as far as the American colonies were concerned, Newport still contained more military excitement than Pennsylvania and New Jersey. Privateers had been outfitted in her port and sent out to cruise against His Majesty's enemies. Privateering vessels sailed proudly back into Narragansett Bay convoying captured prize ships, and the spoils of war made many richer. The tensions and dangers and excitements of England's struggle for supremacy of the seas kept Newport atremble.

The scene Woolman returned to in Newport swept everything else out of his mind. Wealthy merchants, many of them Quakers, were making fortunes out of their trade with the West Indies in sugar and molasses, and hand in hand with that cargo went human cargo. Woolman had known this much, but when he learned that a large shipment of slaves came in to Newport and was being offered for sale by members of the Society, he had to take hold of something to steady himself.

"My appetite failed, and I grew outwardly weak!"

This was the kind of shock experience that could electrify John Woolman into action. Out of his failing appetite, his trembling, his sense of horror, had to come clarity of thought and forthrightness of action.

He entered the meeting hall with the same sense of urgency that he had entered the meeting hall in Burlington and sat immersed in the worship. This Yearly Meeting had not reached the degree of progress in its thinking on slavery where it could be moved by gentle and compassionate words. A completely different kind of approach was needed here, and he did not yet know what it was. He felt at something of a disadvantage, since he did not know Newport Friends as well as he did those in the Yearly Meeting for Pennsylvania and New Jersey.

All through the first day's sessions, during the recesses, at committee meetings, he listened, talked, asked, thought out loud with New England Friends about slavery, because he was groping, searching, praying, yearning for a way to approach the question that would be acceptable. He knew he could rally around him the purist minority, men like Thomas Hazard.

"This trade is a great evil," he argued, "and tends to multiply your troubles, and to bring distresses on the people of these parts."

During the afternoon session of the second day, the inspiration for which Woolman had been praying came to him. Yet, however much he was exercised, he hesitated to proceed until he was confident of his direction.

"On going to bed I got no sleep till my mind was wholly resigned thereto."

At next morning's session he asked a Friend, "How much longer will the General Assembly of Rhode Island be in session?"

It met right there in Newport, and he was assured that it would continue to meet for a few days more.

"It would be well," he suggested, "for Friends to petition the Assembly for a law to discourage the future importation of slaves."

He wrote a draft of a petition himself and showed it to several Friends. There would be difficulties about going to the Assembly, some told him. Others presented reasonable objections to it. But God had planted in John Woolman's mind the idea of going to the Assembly, and an idea of divine origin would not be argued down. When the question of slavery was opened in the business session, he arose to speak:

"I have been under a concern for some time on account of the great number of slaves which are imported into this colony. I am aware that it is a tender point to speak to, but apprehend I am not clear in the sight of Heaven without speaking to it. I have prepared an essay of a petition to be presented to the Legislature, if way open; and what I have to propose to this Meeting is that some Friends may be named to withdraw and look over it, and report whether they believe it suitable to be read in the Meeting. If they should think well of reading it, it will remain for the Meeting to consider whether to take any further notice of it, as a Meeting, or not."

Friends were not liable to ignore the recommendation of a minister of John Woolman's weight, and so the essay was given to a committee.

"Thou hast acted well," said Samuel Eastburn as they waited for the report of the committee.

"Conditions are such here that we could take only a worldly course to the problem," said Woolman; and in a little flurry of excitement he asked wistfully of his friend, "Dost thou believe they will accept it?"

Samuel Eastburn only nodded encouragement and did not offend Woolman's modesty by pointing out that he was a man with an irresistible glow, that words spoken even casually came from his lips radiant and compelling.

The committee returned soon after, recommending that the essay be considered by the Yearly Meeting, and John Woolman sat back and heard his essay read. Some liked it so well they rose and suggested that Woolman's petition to the Assembly be developed more fully. Many were frankly in unity with it, but not the entire Meeting. That was all right, though; it was progress. New England Yearly Meeting had acted on slavery in the past; it could ultimately be persuaded to do so again. As far back as 1717 this Yearly Meeting had asked merchants to "write their correspondents in the West Indies and elsewhere to discourage their sending any more slaves in order to be sold here." The final decision in 1760 was that the petition be signed out of Meeting by as many Friends as cared to do so.

Thomas Hazard rushed to John Woolman and clasped his hand. With a petition signed by sufficient Friends he would be on the spot to carry the fight to the Rhode Island Legislature after Woolman had left.

By the time the Yearly Meeting had come to a close, John Woolman realized that he had stirred New England consciences sufficiently to produce positive action, and he took happy farewells of them all—appetite restored.

Before he left Newport, though, he decided that it would be wise to talk to a few of the wealthier plantation owners in the area, and he consulted with one of the elders. Out of consideration for Woolman's time and energy, a meeting was gathered together in one place, and Woolman spoke to them frankly and directly.

John Woolman's capacity for humility and the training in love and self-restraint that all Friends enjoy held the conference to its "calm and peaceable spirit." He stood before men of wealth asking them to surrender that wealth, and the radiance which he didn't realize he possessed glowed brighter as he felt them respond to his appeal. Some decided then and there to free their slaves in their wills; others showed plainly that their thinking had been altered by his words.

"I am humbly thankful to God, who supported my soul and preserved me in a good degree of resignation through these trials," Woolman wrote in his *Journal* after that hopeful conference.

Weariness? Dangers of travel? Rough forest trails? Choppy

boat crossings? What were they in the face of all he had accomplished? This was the most fruitful religious journey he had ever undertaken!

Soon it would be over, and soon he could turn his horse homeward toward his farmlands, his wife, his daughter, the comforts of his own room.

"We cannot return home without visiting Nantucket," he and Eastburn agreed, and so they joined with some other Friends of New England, visiting meetings en route along Buzzard's Bay, finally setting sail for the island.

It was a happy time amidst the free, independent, proud atmosphere of seafaring folk who had no place in their lives for slavekeeping and exaggerated wealth.

After a few days he and Eastburn bade the Nantucket Friends farewell and sailed back to the mainland, choosing a return route through Connecticut so that they could visit meetings at Greenwich, Shanticut, Warwick, and Oblong. When they reached Flushing and Rahway, Woolman allowed himself to admit that he was homesick.

The journey had been long, full four months, and the trees in his orchard told him that it was August when he rode through his own gate and up the path to his front door.

Mary saw him first and ran down the path, grabbing at the rein as she danced up and down for joy. Sarah stood happily in the doorway, obviously in good health.

"Thou art back," she said softly.

"It was a rewarding journey," he assured her as he put his arm around her and they entered the house together.

19

CONSPICUOUS DRESS

It had indeed been a rewarding journey, but an exhausting journey, too, and there needed to follow a time of solitude and meditation and writing, a time of recovering composure disturbed by being constantly on the move, and a time of restoring health upset by the exertions of travel, a time of reviewing all the family responsibilities that had been neglected.

John Woolman sat at his writing table, looking through his papers, and his hand came upon his "Considerations on the Keeping of Negroes." He reread it only to discover that it was incomplete. His whole perspective had been expanded by the traveling he had been doing. He had seen more slavery, more fruits of human greed; and there was more to be added to the original message. Among his papers were notes and short paragraphs that he had set down from time to time, and he began to shape them all into Part II of "Considerations . . ."

He was discovering that he himself, at the age of forty, did not have the limitless energy and endurance that he had had at twenty. "I am not so hearty and healthy as I have been sometimes," he confessed. The crude ways of travel and the miles on horseback had taxed him to the limit. He needed the balance of the fall and winter to mend physically and spiritually, and he did no more traveling until the spring, confining himself to his own family and immediate neighbors, looking after his younger brothers, his mother's affairs, and his lands. But he did not seem to mend spiritually. Inside of him somewhere was developing a disturbance that he could not quite understand or solve. It disturbed his sleep, distracted him during the day, would not be dispelled by prayer and self-discipline.

Even though he was not completely at peace with himself, he began early in May to visit local meetings again—in Haddonfield and across the river in Pennsylvania—and to wait upon slaveowners and reason with them. It helped him somewhat to know he was attending to his responsibilities, and gave him some inward peace.

Only from time to time, though. The frailties of mankind weighed upon John Woolman with increasing heaviness, and he began to suspect that he himself might be resisting some duty. That meant resisting God, which no man dared do. Perhaps it was within him: the self that loved the gaiety of taverns, the comforts of worldly wealth, the easiness of living only for oneself and one's immediate family.

He tried to write about it: "Under a heavenly covering I have asked my gracious Father to give me a heart in all things resigned to the direction of His wisdom . . ."

And in his own language he found what could be the key.

The phrase "heavenly covering" made him think of physical covering, and when he thought of his physical covering, "the thought of wearing hats and garments dyed with a dye injurious to them" and a whole new anguish began to form: the dye in clothing.

Somehow the idea persisted in his mind, and the dye used in clothing took on a wicked aspect. It was, he thought, a custom not founded in pure wisdom. Somewhere on an almost subconscious level it tied in with his thinking on the sufferings of mankind, slave and free; slaves on indigo plantations, free men wearing garments whose dye was injurious to them.

Would he be serving God's best interest, would he be giving testimony to divine guidance, by wearing undyed clothing? He would be rendering himself conspicuous in his own community if he wore odd dress, and that in itself was an un-Quakerly act, because it was immodest. Yet a man could betray his beliefs by cowardly conformity to custom. The keeping of slaves was itself a cowardly conformity.

Once again he had reached a point where he could not make a moral decision without living through a period of suffering, and while he was enduring his moral suffering he was stricken with an illness. A raging temperature and an aching body took him to bed, just as it had when he was seventeen. This second attack was more serious and of longer duration, and it struck a Woolman who had lost the resilience of youth.

He tossed about on his pillow for a full week, sick in mind and body, tormented by confused visions and phantoms, until the fever passed its highest point and began to recede. Free of his delirium but still hot and dry-mouthed, he tried to understand why he had been stricken.

"One day there was a cry raised in me that I might understand the cause why I was afflicted and improve under it, and my conformity to some customs which I believed were not right was brought to my remembrance."

His indecision about wearing undyed clothing! His shrinking from being thought odd by his own community!

Even understanding could not bring him to the point of deciding, and he lay a long time without the will to recover, since recovery meant facing what had to be. At last, when he felt himself "sinking down into a calm resignation," when he had reached the point of surrender, he experienced with it an inward healing and a gradual return of strength.

Health and strength and resignation to the will of God totaled happiness for Woolman. Somehow he would find within himself the fortitude to live without those who would fall away from him in the face of his new determination to wear undyed clothing. A few Friends would surely understand that it was not of his own design or will.

He was up before very much longer, strolling about in the warm June air. He had said nothing about his decision to anyone; he wasn't sure he would be able to explain it to anyone. First things first. He must get back his full strength, and later he would make definite plans for his wardrobe.

He strolled as far as the Woolman farm in Rancocas one day, to test his strength, and was pleased to discover that the five miles had tired him very little. There in the house where he himself had been a child he sank into a familiar chair to chat with his mother.

There was plenty of quiet now for conversation. No longer did thirteen children make a hubbub. Rachel, the youngest girl, was the only daughter still at home and unwed. Asher was still a bachelor.

Elizabeth Woolman looked at this most extraordinary of all her sons. How far he had grown and developed! What an important place he occupied in the Society of Friends! She could detect not a trace of the "wanton" boy. His seasoned face was sweet and kindly, brimming with an abundance of sympathy.

A twinkle of mischief lighted her eyes as she said, "Thou canst advise me on a moral question, my son."

A little smile disturbed his lips at the suggestion. Elizabeth Woolman had born him and diapered him, had taught him to walk and rebuked his misdeeds, had lived with him through all of his growing pains, and had advised him on raising his own children.

"Is it perhaps about the property?" he asked.

"No," said she primly. "I said this is a moral question," and turning to her daughter she added, "Bring it to me, Rachel."

Rachel looked a little afraid.

"John will disapprove, Mother," she protested.

"I told thee to bring it to me, Rachel."

Rachel obeyed and laid the mysterious item in her mother's lap. John Woolman recognized it as something he had seen in the New England cities he had just visited. It was a bonnet, a fashion note from Paris, the wickedest city in the world, where the infamy and chicanery of Madame Pompadour and her circle had helped to precipitate the Seven Years' War. The bonnet in Elizabeth Woolman's lap was a plain replica of the ornate original. Quaker women in England had already been wearing the bonnet for some time in spite of the severe disapproval of their meetings.

If there was any mortal in the New World able to face up to the disapproval of John Woolman it was John Woolman's mother.

With hands upon which the skin hung loose and wrinkled she picked up the bonnet, placed it snugly on her head, and tied it under her chin, waiting as pertly as a coquette for his comment.

The righteous man who had just made such a harrowing decision about his own costume nodded in the affirmative and said:

"I think it becomes thee, Mother. I really do."

20

AMONG THE WARRING INDIANS

He looked over his wardrobe very soon after and discovered that he owned many items of dyed clothing that were still entirely wearable. He was incapable of willful waste; so he decided to replace each piece as it wore out with another of undyed fabric. Only his hat was worn enough to discard, and with considerable self-consciousness John Woolman purchased another, a beaver "the natural color of the fur."

Finding a white beaver hat was easy enough then, because white beavers were much in demand by light-headed, gay, and fast-living young dandies. They were a frank avowal of wantonness. For a weighty Friend, a minister and elder, to walk into Meeting for Worship wearing a white beaver hat without any advance word of explanation was courting criticism, stares, and loss of respect.

Sarah either understood or pretended to, and she appeared

in public by her husband's side with the same gentle dignity with which she accepted every other phase of her life with John Woolman. The design or color of a man's hat did not determine his character, just so his head be covered at the proper times.

But John Woolman's spirit suffered from the shyness of his friends. They had a right to know why he had adopted a conspicuous way of dress.

"Some Friends were apprehensive that my wearing such a hat savoured of an affected singularity; those who spoke with me in a friendly way I generally informed in a few words, that I believed my wearing it was not in my own will."

He gradually replaced one garment after another, and by the time the General Spring Meeting of 1762 rolled around he was garbed in white. He caused a stir there, of course; but after the first shock his closest associates began to accept this new singularity. After all, they had known the real Woolman since childhood. His familiar figure walking or riding along the Jersey highways was as familiar as ever and a little easier to see at a distance in his white raiment.

There were other matters for Friends to give their thought to, and their scrupulous sense of values turned their attention to the affairs of the world. The political picture in England had changed. George II had died in 1760 and George III had taken his place on the throne. The war had been dragging on for so many years that the participants were spent and weary, and by the end of another year the Treaty of Paris brought the whole costly affair to an end. France was through as a world power; she had lost her foothold in India and all of her American colonies except a few scattered islands. Spain had become involved toward the end, and although she let Florida go to England she emerged as owner of the western part of the Mississippi Valley known as Louisiana. Great Britain emerged supreme, mistress of the high seas, dominant power in India, and ruler of most of North America.

Woolman was living through a period of withdrawal from his usual intimacies with people. He sensed the widespread disapproval of his odd dress, probably exaggerated it in his own hypersensitive mind, and found his adjustment to it more difficult than he had imagined it would be. He really didn't entirely understand his own motives. Somehow, the dyes in fabrics were related to rich living and exploitation and greed.

But John Woolman's devotion to the "everlasting welfare of his fellow creatures" gradually crowded self-consciousness out of his thinking. The French and Indian War had stimulated his interest in Indian problems as it had others. During the last year or so of the war, as Woolman met Indians in Philadelphia and talked to travelers back from the frontiers, he began to experience the ambition to go among the Indians himself. He met some Indians who lived on the east branch of the Susquehanna River at a camp called Wehaloosing. After talking with them he felt real "drawings" to visit Wehaloosing and carry the Friends' message to the Indians dwelling there.

He plunged his Monthly Meeting into consternation when he announced his intent.

"Wait a few months, John Woolman! Postpone thy journey!"

The Treaty of Paris was signed in February, 1763, but those who drew up the treaty—Great Britain, France, and Spain—forgot to consult the Indians of North America, even though the Indians had been considered worthy enough to be dealt with when their military support was needed. As one Indian chieftain sorrowfully summed it up, "You English and

French are like two edges of a pair of shears. We are the cloth, which is cut to pieces between them."

Indian tempers did not turn off like a faucet. Their loves and loyalties and hatreds were more real than that. A great majority of the Indians had been won over to the side of the French during the French and Indian War, and they were not prepared to switch allegiance to the British victors. Many in the outer reaches of the wilderness did not believe that such a victory had taken place.

Pontiac was chief of the Ottawas, who dwelt in the land around Saginaw Bay which is now Michigan. The Ottawas lived in the cold country and had the richest furs to trade. They had been reached long ago by the French traders and the Jesuit Fathers. Pontiac was a powerful leader with influence over other tribes as well as his own, among them the Ojibways and Pottawatomies. The French had always paid him appropriate homage, respected his judgment, and enlisted his aid in wartime. When Duquesne, Ticonderoga, Niagara, Quebec—and all of Canada—fell to the English, Pontiac knew that his people were in grave danger of being driven off still more of their lands. Pontiac, the great, the proud, the powerful, the revered chieftain, knew that the responsibility rested with him. So he decided to wage a war that would drive the English into the sea.

The idea appealed to the Indians of many tribes; the whole Algonquin nation joined him. Pontiac's first major attack was against Detroit, and the siege was long and bloody and tragic, dragging on from early May into the summer, while other Indian tribes attacked in other places. In May they seized Fort Sandusky on the southern rim of Lake Erie, killing the entire garrison except the ensign in charge. They were advancing against points all along the western borders of Pennsylvania and New York. Fort after fort on the Great Lakes fell to their hands, and only Detroit was holding out. As the Indians penetrated into Pennsylvania they enlisted the Delawares and other local tribes and attacked Fort Pitt, the fort guarding Pittsburgh. By June the Shawnees joined in the war against the English; so did the Senecas of New York.

Once again terror spread along the western frontiers.

"The Indians are on the warpath, John Woolman! Please do not go among them now!"

With some honest misgivings, with "inward breathings for heavenly support," with thoughts often attended with "unusual sadness," John Woolman continued to make plans for his journey among the Indians. Advice was plentiful about the foolhardiness of his plans, but he would not change his mind. He would meet his Indian guide at Samuel Foulke's house in Richland (Quakertown) on the seventh day of June.

News of Indian atrocities kept coming in from the frontiers, and his friends pleaded with him up to the last day. In the middle of the night before his departure, some Friends came knocking on his door and asked him to come to a conference in Mount Holly.

"A group of Friends wishes to speak with thee," he was told.

He hurried into his clothes and joined them, walking down Old Springfield Road in the dark. In a public house he found waiting for him a group of Friends who had just arrived from Philadelphia, and he listened while they told him of Indian atrocities at Pittsburgh. An express rider had reached Philadelphia the day before.

"Indians have taken a fort from the English westward and have slain and scalped some English people. Thou must not continue thy journey."

He considered the advice very carefully, as he always did. Traveling into Pennsylvania when Indians of so many descriptions were aroused to war against the English would not be safe. Woolman was as human as anyone else; he wanted to live; and he liked to feel safe. There were times, though, when responsibilities took a man away from his sources of security, and those times must be met with fortitude.

He thanked his friends and bade them good night. All he could promise was that he would consider their advice.

He returned home and did not tell Sarah about the middle-of-the-night meeting until the next morning. By that time his decision was made: he must make the journey. Sarah helped him pack his saddlebags and stood by while he mounted.

John and Israel Pemberton went with him part of the way, still arguing. The savages in the hills were wild and untamed, they pointed out; when Indians went on the warpath they were not to be reasoned with. He must be sensible. Why could he not go to Wehaloosing when order was restored?

The compulsion in John Woolman's heart was *now*.

They crossed the Delaware to Philadelphia, and the next morning John Pemberton still continued to travel with Woolman as far as Richland in Bucks County, where Samuel Foulke was waiting. The Indian guide and his family were waiting, too; and so was Benjamin Parvin. Woolman was surprised to see Parvin, and his surprise increased when Parvin said: "I have decided to go with thee."

Parvin was seven years Woolman's junior. The other men smiled and nodded their approval. They, frankly, did not feel physically up to any such journey, and they were glad that young Parvin could go.

"I cannot allow thee to go with me," Woolman said flatly to Parvin. "If thou hast come to bear me company and we

should be taken captive, my having been the means by drawing thee into these difficulties would add to my own affliction."

Parvin was blessed with his own share of Quaker stubbornness, and he answered briefly, "My decision has already been
made."

Deep down in his heart, Woolman was grateful for the gesture, and so he yielded and allowed Parvin to travel with him.
Next morning, 9th of the Sixth Month, the real journey
started, and John Pemberton and another Friend went with
Woolman's party as far as Bethlehem. There John Pemberton turned back, and the others went on, leaving the comfort
of towns behind them.

"I am now at Bethlehem, a Moravian town, and midling
well," Woolman wrote in a letter to Sarah that John Pemberton carried back to Philadelphia to post.

The second night Woolman and his companions were per-
mitted to sleep on the floor of a primitive settler's house,
rolled up in their blankets. Here the other Friend turned
back, and Woolman, Parvin, and the Indians went on together, headed for the county that lay in the northernmost
reaches of Pennsylvania.

Next day they settled carefully into canoes and crossed the
Great Lehigh River, a branch of the Delaware, near Fort
Allen. On the opposite side stood a strange Indian watching
them. Since Woolman had no evil motives in his mind and no
deadly weapon in his hand, he stepped from the canoe and
walked with a friendly manner toward the strange red man.
Woolman possessed more than a friendly manner; he glowed
with charm, too. His friendliness and charm were repaid in
kind, and the stranger spoke sufficient English so that they
could exchange thoughts. Woolman and his companions
shared their biscuits with the stranger, and the stranger, who

had just killed a deer, shared his meat with them. Finally the six remounted and resumed their journey through the wilderness.

As they penetrated deeper into the forests they met other Indians from time to time. A group of Indian men and women passed them traveling down from Wyoming (near the present city of Wilkes-Barre) leading a horse and a cow and carrying bundles of belongings. They were moving, they told Woolman and Parvin in English. They were moving out of Wyoming.

"I am traveling into your country to worship the Good Manetta [Good Spirit] with your people," Woolman explained.

They nodded soberly, approving his motives.

"They took leave of us with an appearance of sincere affection," was Woolman's humble observation, after the Indians had passed on their way.

They were so far into the forests by this time that there were no roads except Indian foot trails and the winding streams and creeks. The whisperings and murmurings of the trees, the sudden noises of waterfalls, fleeting shadows in the subdued lighting that might have been animals, Indian scouts, or a traveler's imagination, closed in around the travelers. They came to a stretch of mountain, the Blue Mountain, that had to be crossed to reach the Delaware Valley on the other side. Here in these higher places grew the tall pines and hemlocks, the oaks and the cedar; and here roamed the wildest animals—bears, wolves, and wildcats.

They began their assent up the craggy, rocky side, following the guide as he moved forward with quiet confidence. Often they had to dismount and lead their horses around rocks, over fallen trees, across brooks. Woolman felt his strength taxed to the utmost, as he sometimes found himself on hands and knees dragging himself up over a ledge. He was glad that the younger and more agile Parvin was with him.

Mother nature spared them from wild animals and sent a pouring rain to chasten them instead.

They toiled over Blue Mountain a whole day until it was time to make camp for the night. The ground was wet, and the branches they collected to lay under their blankets were wet. They built a campfire at the door of their tent, but it was feeble comfort. When Woolman awoke the next morning, he found it difficult to arouse his lame and aching body, and as he sat up he was afraid he might actually be ill. Forcing himself to stand, he walked painfully toward the bank of the river that they were still following. God's clear sparkling water! Boon of everything that dwelt in the forest! It could not help but heal him. He removed his clothing and plunged into the chilly stream and soon emerged feeling "fresh and well."

The trees about their temporary camp were grim reminders of the situation in Pennsylvania, for on their peeled trunks the Indians had painted red and black pictures, the only written language many of them knew, telling stories of their men who had passed to and fro along this trail on their way to wars.

John Woolman looked at the lurid pictures and felt himself overwhelmed with a desire to "cherish the spirit of love and peace amongst these people." His desire to bring the message of peace to the Indians became overpowering, causing him to forget his lameness and weariness, even possible danger at the hands of the people whom he sought.

He and his party pushed on, crossing yet another mountain ridge and two swamps. More rain! They pitched their tents and built their fire and beds on the wet ground again. After another day they were overtaken by a Moravian missionary on his way to visit the same Indians at Wehaloosing. He had been to them before, he explained, and the Indians had invited him to return.

The Moravians were another Christian sect living in Pennsylvania who had been working among the Indians for years, bringing them help and comfort, and converting many of them to Christianity.

The Moravian was traveling faster than Woolman and Parvin, and they soon lost him. Woolman was not a competing evangelist, and he made no effort to hasten his own pace. One man could speak for God as eloquently as another.

By the thirteenth of June, Woolman, Parvin, and the guides were riding over barren hills, and Woolman was lost in thought. The natives of this land had been driven back into the hills and away from the more favorable places along the sea. They had been persuaded to sell their inheritances for trifles.

When white people sold rum to the Indians, they were creating a great evil. The Indian had never had any intoxicating beverages in his culture, and when he drank he became quarrelsome, dangerous, and weak. After he had endured physical hardships hunting for pelts in the forest and then brought them down to exchange for food and clothing, he was plied with rum and betrayed into selling his furs for a lower price or for more rum. Yes, the white man had created his own dangers.

Indians had learned to distrust Europeans, Woolman reflected, and he thought of the comforts and prosperity of the English who lived along the coast and of the misery and suffering of Indians and slaves.

He had to bring his reflecting to an abrupt halt as they approached the Indian settlement at Wyoming.

The Indian guide made a gesture and uttered a few syllables to indicate that their journey was almost done. Wehaloosing was just a little farther up the Susquehanna River, he explained.

But Wyoming was directly before them, and it spelled danger.

The Indian village bristled when the white men rode in. War news had been coming in to them, borne by one runner after another. Two days earlier they had learned that Indians had captured one English fort and had begun to attack another. A second messenger had arrived breathlessly from a town near Wehaloosing the day before, reporting that Indian warriors had arrived there wearing English scalps on their belts. Did the white men not understand that this was a time of war against the English? Did they have no more sense than to ride brazenly into Wyoming?

Staying close together, Parvin and Woolman rode to the center of the cluster of wigwams and dismounted, and their guide led them to the dwelling of an ancient man of the village.

Woolman stayed inside the hut only a moment. He could accomplish nothing by hiding there! Outside the door stood a guard, and Woolman stepped out to speak to him. The guard automatically reached for his tomahawk. Woolman moved toward him, both empty hands in plain view, and addressed him in his friendly, humble, gracious manner. The hand on the deadly weapon relaxed, and the guard replied in English. Not even a warring savage could resist the charm of John Woolman.

The news brought by the runners had upset his people, the Indian explained. Their location was dangerous, their numbers small, so they were planning to move en masse somewhere else where there was a larger settlement.

Parvin came out and joined the two men, and the three chatted quietly until dark.

"John Woolman," Parvin pleaded in a low voice, after they had retired for the night, "please reconsider the rest of thy journey."

"We have only a few more miles to go," was all John Woolman said, but he did not admit how deeply troubled he was.

That night he worried and pondered and turned back and forth on his primitive bed, trying to resolve a decision. Why *was* he so determined to go into the wilderness at a time when England and the Indians were at war? Was his intent genuine? Was he truly being obedient to God's will, or was he secretly vain about desiring the reputation of a man who could persevere through dangers? It was difficult for a man to look at himself honestly and know his own subtlest motives.

Daylight brought calmness, and John Woolman visited in several of the Indian homes to explain his mission. "My intent is peaceful," he assured them.

On up the winding Susquehanna River John Woolman and Benjamin Parvin pursued their way. They passed clusters of wigwams now and then. Indians usually built near streams where the trout could be found, where the animals that they needed came to drink, and where they themselves would have water. Often the Quakers stopped and made friends and shared food.

A quick and violent storm struck on the fifteenth, coming right through their tent, soaking them and their baggage. They found the way even more hazardous after the storm; fallen trees blocked their path and long stretches of the trail were turned to swamp.

When Job Chilaway, an Indian from Wehaloosing, appeared on their path, they knew they were nearing their destination. He was on his way downstream to purchase supplies.

"Warriors near Wehaloosing are taking the warpath against the English," he warned them.

Job Chilaway had been to Philadelphia many times. He spoke fluent English and he knew the Friends, because he had sometimes acted as interpreter at conferences. When he realized that Woolman did not intend to heed his warning, he delayed his own journey and retraced his steps about six miles to aid the travelers.

John Woolman's conscience was suffering fresh anguish, and when this combined with the fatigues of the journey, a wave of nausea swept through him. Torture, exposure, scalping, burning, dismembering—all or any could be their fate; and he had brought young Benjamin Parvin into this danger out of sheer stubbornness.

Job Chilaway could not stay with them long, and he soon turned back downstream and left the travelers to their fate. He carried two of Woolman's letters with him, one to Israel Pemberton—"We are now well near Wehaloosing in company with Job Chilaway. . . ." —and one to Sarah— "My dear and tender wife, A sense of alsufficiency of God in supporting those who trust in Him . . . feels comfortable to me in my journey. . . ."

Later that same day, a Wehaloosing woman with a baby strapped to her back met them on the path. Wehaloosing had been alerted, she warned them; the whole village was waiting to receive them.

When she had disappeared from sight, Parvin spoke once more, "John Woolman, please consider . . ."

Woolman clasped his hand. "Too little have I considered thy safety and welfare, Benjamin Parvin."

Their Indian guide instructed them to wait where they were. He would go ahead to the village.

Parvin and Woolman rested upon a log, "sitting thus together in a deep inward stillness . . ."

They lifted their heads suddenly when the shrill, penetrating tones of a conch shell blown several times startled them. That was the signal. They were to proceed to the village.

Together they walked into the settlement, and it seemed deserted. About forty houses, "some thirty feet long, some bigger, were built mostly of split plank and covered with bark." This was Wehaloosing on the bank of the Susquehanna, but where were its inhabitants?

The Quakers were led into one of the houses. There, waiting for them, were some sixty Indians, sitting on the ground in silence, prepared to commune with the Good Spirit as soon as their visitors joined them.

Scalpings? Torture? No! These people were assembled in worship!

With a sudden leap of his heart Woolman surveyed the gentle scene and recognized some of its members. There was their chief, Papunehang, who had come down to Philadelphia many times for peace conferences and had visited in Anthony Benezet's house. The proud and dignified Chief Papunehang stepped forward and welcomed his Quaker visitors, escorting them to their places.

Exchanging one happy glance, Woolman and Parvin sat down among the worshipers and entered into the silence with them. It was a profoundly successful meeting, because the Indians were natural mystics, and John Woolman was soon on his feet speaking out of the depths of his heart, conveying his tenderness even to those who did not understand his language.

The Moravian missionary was there among the Indians, and as soon as the meeting was over, John Woolman went to him and spoke:

"Since thou hast already established meetings here, I have no wish to establish others; but may I attend thy meetings and speak there when love engages me to do so?"

Of course! The Moravian extended his hand. He had indeed established meetings, and had long since converted many of these Delawares, including Chief Papunehang, to Christianity.

The next evening another meeting took place.

"Pure gospel love was felt, to the tendering of some of our hearts," Woolman recorded. "The interpreters endeavoured to acquaint the people of what I said in short sentences, but found some difficulty, as none of them were quite perfect in the English and Delaware tongues, so they helped one another and we laboured along."

After the rise of the meeting, one of the Delawares uttered some words in his own language, and Woolman asked one of the interpreters to explain.

The man had said, "I love to feel where words come from."

21

PRECIOUS HABITATION

John Woolman remained with the Delawares for five days, his heart "filled with heavenly care for their good." In meeting after meeting as they worshiped together in two languages, often understanding one another's intent without benefit of translation, Woolman, Chief Papunehang, or the Moravian would rise to his feet and pray aloud.

"Though I had the same dangerous wilderness between me and home, I was inwardly joyful that the Lord had strengthened me to come on this visit, and manifested a fatherly care over me in my poor lowly condition, when, in my own eyes, I appeared inferior to many amongst the Indians."

Their final meeting together seemed to Woolman to be the most successful of all; he found in it a profound reassurance that the message of peace and love that he had brought would bear rich fruit in the future, and felt at liberty to return home, mission accomplished.

"Thou hast been a needed companion," he said to Parvin as they started on their return journey.

A large group of Delawares, who were going down to Bethlehem with skins and furs to sell, accompanied them back over the perilous route.

Over the Blue Mountain, back down the long trail that was so vague in spots that only the Indians could find it.

"We forded the westerly branch of the Delaware three times, and thereby had missed the highest part of the Blue Mountains called the Second Ridge."

When they drew near Bethlehem, Woolman and Parvin were able to protect their Indian friends in turn by walking ahead of them as they approached white settlements, explaining their peaceable intent. Hysteria of fear stalked the land as reports kept coming in from the west about the Indian war against the English.

Benjamin Parvin bade Woolman farewell at Samuel Foulke's house, and Samuel Foulke, with a happy sigh at seeing Woolman alive and safe, joined him and rode with him for a few miles.

"John Woolman has returned!" The news traveled among the Friends of Philadelphia, Burlington, and Mount Holly.

"John Woolman traveled through the wilderness and met the Indians peaceably!"

"John Woolman is safe and well!"

"John Woolman will be at Meeting to report on his journey!"

Sarah threw open the door to him once more and indulged her own little smile of relief. She alone knew how tired and spent he really was. She prepared him a hot bath, laid out clean clothing, and set before him the kind of food to which his stomach was accustomed.

It was Woolman's physical body that needed rest. His soul

labored on in the history of his times. Pontiac's war was driving eastward, still laying siege to Detroit and Pittsburgh, threatening settlers' lives as far as New Jersey. But early in August troops fought their way through two major encounters with the Indians to enter Fort Pitt, which ended the crisis in western Pennsylvania, and the siege of Detroit was raised in October. The French in Illinois were striving for peace as much as the English, and when Pontiac realized that he was waging a losing fight, that he could not prevent reinforcements from reaching the forts, he capitulated. The peace treaty between the French and English had been more binding than he had believed. So by late fall peace in the colonies was a reality.

Pontiac's war had reopened and kept alive the questions of war taxes and military service, and Woolman added these to the other burdens of his heart. They were a part of the continuous prayer that flowed through him. During July, before either Pitt or Detroit had been liberated, he was visited by another of his dreams.

He was on a religious journey, in his dream, somewhere beyond the seas, and the country he was visiting went to war with a nearby kingdom. There was only a line between the two countries, and the enemy chief lived only a short distance away. Engaging a guide, Woolman set out to visit the enemy leader, "and after traveling sometime in the woods we came in sight of a few of those people at labour having guns with them." Woolman ignored the guns and shook hands, explaining his peaceable intent. He was then led through woods and swamps to the home of the chief, "the head of the affairs of their country but was not called a king." Woolman was not only received by the leader, but was invited to dinner, too, and just as he was about to explain his business he awoke, leaving the whole affair unfinished.

Why beyond the sea when his life was in Mount Holly? Where was the neighboring kingdom? This dream seemed to have about it a quality of his beloved Book of Revelation, full of double meanings and symbols. Why had he not been allowed to finish his business? What was left undone?

"Your teacher is within you," George Fox had said.

The disturbance that had begun within John Woolman a year or more earlier and had caused him to adopt undyed dress was not quieted by his unfinished dream. It drove him to seek harder after a personal perfection and a purity that kept eluding him. But while his personality and manner seemed to grow more eccentric as time passed, his lovable qualities grew no less. To his family and neighbors he was simply taking on odd little mannerisms and an odd appearance. He seemed more detached, preoccupied, turned inward, not always hearing what was said to him unless his attention was secured first.

He began to speak censoriously of any worldiness of which he disapproved. When he heard that a juggler had come to a Mount Holly public house and was gathering crowds around him with sleight-of-hand tricks, he investigated and told the crowd there were more fruitful and constructive ways to spend their money and their time. When he went to Yearly Meeting and saw the costly furnishings in the homes of some of the city-dwelling Friends, his disapproval was frank and tinged with prophesy.

Everyone with whom he dealt seemed to shatter his peace of mind. Even a hired man who had come to work on his farmland told him one evening the story of his experiences in the French and Indian War. He had been taken captive with some others and had had to watch his companions tortured to death.

Woolman took refuge in his pen, late at night. "Doth pride
lead to vanity? Doth vanity form imaginary wants? . . . Does
malice, when ripe, become revengeful, and in the end in-
flict terrible pains on our fellow creatures and spread desola-
tion in the world?"

Where was peace? It was certainly not within Woolman except in degree, and he could not seem to realize that a world
peopled with John Woolmans could have known peace. He
had within himself a newly growing disturbance, a renewed
searching and seeking, and he struggled with it for the next
several years.

He tried a new avenue of service: schoolteaching. He had
dwelt deep in his mind upon children and young people and
the responsibility of the adult world in handing on the faith
to them. He had watched carefully over the education of his
daughter, now in her teens. His essay "On Schools" had been
written before Part II of "Considerations. . . ."

He opened a school "for Friends' children and others," and
when a child could not afford his own spelling book or writing material or powder to dry his ink, John Woolman furnished them himself. When a youngster needed a coat . . .
well . . . John Woolman was a tailor. In due time he composed a primer of his own, A First Book for Children. Beginning with the alphabet, it led the beginner through the
building of one-syllable words to the construction of simple
sentences.

His outward life through the winter months became rather
sedentary, devoted to sewing and teaching, allowing him a
chance to recover some of his physical strength. His inward
life was torn.

Slavery still called him. Memories of conditions on slave
plantations still haunted him. He had reached a few with his

message on each of his journeys southward, perhaps he could have reached more if he had been more humble, more lowly. A new facet of his mind caught a ray and flashed it to his heart. Traveling on foot could well be the way to set an "example of lowliness before the eyes of the slave masters."

He was alive with new purpose! He would go on a walking journey among the Friends on the eastern shore of Maryland. He would expiate their sins for them, before their very eyes, by going on foot in the dust and the heat.

Consternation spread through Mount Holly when his newest plan came to light, and again, as on the Indian journey, a younger man who could stand the rigors of the trip better than the forty-six-year-old Woolman announced that he was going along. The man was John Sleeper, a neighbor who earned his living as a carpenter.

"It is well that John Sleeper is going, because we cannot dissuade John Woolman."

On the sixth of May, 1766, the two Friends set out to Wilmington, Duck Creek, Little Creek, and Motherkill; then thirty-five miles to Tuckahoe in Maryland. Woolman was amazed and comforted to meet a preacher named Joseph Nichols, who preached ardently against slavery and whose followers would wear no dye in their clothing. He trudged on in the hot southern sun from meeting to meeting down the eastern shore of Chesapeake Bay, as far as Queen Anne, preaching, needling consciences, praying.

When Friends saw him they would be appalled and embarrassed by his utter humility, and they would plead:

"Thou shouldst have a horse, John Woolman!"

He shook his head, even though the lack of a horse was taking a severe toll of his strength. He was enduring these discomforts to atone for the sins of his fellow men.

The days were hot and dry and he began to "grow weakly."

"We must travel more slowly," he gasped with a note of discouragement. "I've been too anxious to be on with it."

"We must stop and rest altogether," John Sleeper insisted, and enforced his advice before they turned back.

Mile by mile they at last made their way back up the eastern shore, visiting meetings they had missed on the way down, until at last they reached home.

Woolman's own fatigue had given him a real understanding of the lot of the slave who must labor incessantly in the hot sun and never be allowed to say, "We must travel more slowly." He knew he had moved some slaveholders to a better understanding, and the knowledge brought him a little closer to happiness, eased his own mind for a while. Only in utter humility, the simple unworldy humility of a child, could a man find peace.

By another spring the other shore of Chesapeake Bay began to stir him, and April saw him planning a second walking mission. This was the trip he called his "lonesome walk," because he went without any companion.

John Woolman clad in white! John Woolman wandering alone, through the long, uninhabited forest trails, along dusty roads, through towns and hamlets! Growing weak and weary, sometimes almost crushed by the sorrow he felt for his fellow creatures, for their pride and wantonness, for their selfishness and greed, for their cruel disregard for others!

When his strength failed altogether, he would sit by the side of the road and seek a brief communion with God. Then on he would go to treat congregations to his eloquence and individuals to his fervent pleading.

"I found peace, and the sincere-hearted were comforted."

Exhausted, spent both physically and spiritually, he turned back toward Pennsylvania.

The increasing slavery, the "condition of the church" in

the South, drew him a third time; and in the summer of 1768 he went once more into Maryland and Delaware without a horse.

Slavery would not let him rest.

His tiring walking trips through the slave colonies had stirred him so deeply that from his deepest consciousness there rose a gnawing memory—the Negro boy he had once long ago placed with a kindly master when he was an executor of a will. Perhaps that was the cause of his unrest. Perhaps it was that wrong deed of his *own* against the Negro people that denied him final peace. The boy could not have his freedom until he was thirty, and that would be in 1775. Another seven years of servitude!

A vivid, unforgivable sin, the deed stood out in John Woolman's mind until he realized that it required some atonement, a definite act that would expiate the wrong.

"I might be resigned to go on a visit to some part of the West Indies . . ."

The very idea of such a journey was sobering. Travel in the West Indies guaranteed risks and dangers all its own. Others had gone to the West Indies and succumbed to the climate or to tropical diseases. If that were the expiation that God expected of him, then his sin against the Negro boy, James, had been grievous indeed.

John Woolman found himself back on a level with the carefree boy whom God had called. He must make a decision, and he did not immediately have the courage to make it. He knew better than anyone else how his health was fading. His body simply would not do as much for him as it had ten or fifteen or twenty years earlier, and it was expressing its protest at being overtaxed. There was a growing lump on the side of his nose that Woolman was trying to overcome with severe dieting. The dieting had no effect on the lump and only left him with lowered resistance.

"Covered with darkness and sorrow," he turned to his source of absolute wisdom, to God in solitude, to wait upon Him and to beg direction. Gradually it became clear that there were two phases to his wrong deed: the past which could not be undone, and the future, the additional years that James must serve. Since Woolman was one of two executors, he could legally redeem one half of the boy's remaining years of servitude. So he drew the necessary papers promising that he would pay to the man who owned James sufficient money to cover the last three years and a half of James' time.

There remained the past and whether a trip to the West Indies would make up for having sold James in the first place. If he went to the West Indies, he would probably go to British-owned Barbados, farthest away, most tropical, less than fifteen degrees from the equator. The first Friends to reach America a hundred years earlier had landed at Barbados. George Fox had come there shortly after, and by Woolman's time there were large Meetings on the sugar-producing, slave-using island.

Fighting a deep reluctance, Woolman went ahead with his plans for a trip. He obtained certificates from his Monthly and Quarterly Meetings, purchased a "sea-store and bed and things fitting for a voyage," and, hearing of a ship likely to sail from Philadelphia for Barbados, he spoke to the owner, who lived in Burlington.

Going through the motions of making commitments and plans helped his resolution, but not sufficiently. The West Indies—the whole Caribbean situation—preyed on his mind. It was an area of trading in rum, sugar, molasses, the fruits of slave labor, and the vessel on which he was to embark was active in this trade. Then another flash of light: Ought he to sail in a ship engaged in the carrying of slave products?

"If such doubts assail me, my direction isn't clear," he thought.

He lived in a turmoil and torment trying to know what was right to do. He believed his mind was resigned to the assignment of going to the West Indies, but he did not feel a "clearness to proceed."

Suddenly a phrase from the New Testament occurred to him: "Take no thought for the morrow." That was his answer; take no thought for the morrow. The vessel would not sail for several days. Why did he not simply tarry in town until the sailing date arrived?

The date arrived, and the vessel sailed—without John Woolman. With a deep sense of relief and comfort he returned to his home in Mount Holly.

"But I still felt like a sojourner with my family."

Discontented, dissatisfied with himself, feeling that he had another mission ahead of him, he felt detached from his own world and from his own life.

He was stricken with pleurisy toward the end of December, and he lay for days in pain and fever. Three nurses hovered over him: his wife and his daughter and his daughter's sweetheart, John Comfort. Neighbors came and went, and so did relatives from Mount Holly, Rancocas, and Peachfields. They watched closely and with little hope as he sank into delirium and as his strength dwindled. For a long time he struggled and prayed to live, thinking the illness had been sent to "further refine" him; but eventually he began to give messages to this one and that, to call one or another to his bedside so that he could dictate final thoughts.

On First Day he wanted a Meeting for Worship, and a

group of neighbors came to his bedside, John Sleeper and his wife among them.

John Woolman sank lower after that Meeting, until one night he reached the low point of his ailment and himself gave up thoughts of recovery. His feet had turned cold and he could feel the cold increasing in his legs.

But death was not yet.

Through a torment of visions distorted by fever, some memories, some the products of his imagination, John Woolman reached the depths of weakness and entered into one of his rare intimacies with God. So close to death that he felt his extremities turning cold, yet with life retained, he breathed faintly, eyes closed, and felt himself suspended in "the spring of pure love." Such a fragile moment that even those at his bedside could not have known.

Without opening his eyes he whispered to Mary to wrap something warm around his feet. He was going to live! A little later he asked someone in attendance to write down the experience: "I have seen in the Light . . . that the day is approaching when the man that is most wise shall be the greatest fool . . ."

He was not out of danger, and there was another lapse into torment, when in spite of his weakness he rose up to his feet and cried from a dry, hoarse throat for mercy because he had "given up the purity of his testimony against the West India trade." The specter of slavery pursued him even in illness.

He recovered slowly, but by the middle of January, 1770, he was able to sit up in bed, a hopeful convalescent, and to a weighty Friend seated by his side he dictated this paragraph:

"The place of prayer is a precious habitation; for I now saw that the prayers of saints were precious incense; and a trumpet was given to me that I might sound forth this language; that the children might hear it and be invited together to this precious habitation. . . . I saw this habitation to be safe,—to be inwardly quiet when there were great stirrings and commotions in the world."

22

THE MISSION ABROAD

Inward quiet is vital substance of Friends' doctrine, inward quiet where sober, compassionate thinking can be done and wise decisions made no matter how violent the affairs of the world.

The colonies were being drawn back into the affairs of the world with mounting tensions and shortening tempers as George III proved to be less understanding and more autocratic than his predecessor. England was deeply in debt as a result of the Seven Years' War, and she looked to her colonies to produce profitable trade and taxes to pay off that debt. In the first year after the war had come the Sugar Act, that taxed sugar imported by the colonies from anywhere except British possessions; and the Currency Act, that would not allow the colonies to issue their own paper currency. The year 1765 brought the Stamp Act, which was intended to raise money to meet the costs of governing the colonies and required a government stamp upon legal papers, merchants' licenses, college diplomas, newspapers, and an almost endless list of other items.

On the heels of the Stamp Act came the Quartering Act, forcing colonists to provide food and lodging for British soldiers sent to America to enforce these new acts. But it was the Stamp Act that set off the loudest protests and united the colonies even more than the French and Indian War had done. Sons and Daughters of Liberty were organized to campaign against the purchase of the stamps. Crowds rioted in the streets, from Boston to Charleston. In a few months delegates from nine of the colonies met in New York as the Stamp Act Congress and drew up a formal protest to Parliament declaring that colonists were entitled to the same liberties and representations as other British subjects. So strong was the protest and so dangerous did the situation become that Parliament repealed the Stamp Act the following year.

But with amazing lack of wisdom came another act declaring that the British Parliament had the right to make laws governing the colonies. Then came customs and revenue acts regulating and restricting the trade of the colonies to give the mother country the maximum benefit. They were followed by the first of two fatal Tea Acts granting the British East India Company a monopoly on tea business in America.

Woolman had experienced his prophetic dream in 1764 about parties preparing for a general war. In March, 1770, when he was still feeling lingering effects of his illness, the news of a tragic street scene in Boston flew over the post roads. British soldiers who were stationed there were harassed and stoned by a rowdy group of men and boys. The soldiers fired into the crowd, and five were killed and half a dozen others wounded. The incident enflamed public opinion, and it was soon being called the "Boston Massacre."

Neither John Woolman nor the rest of the Friends needed to be prophets to foresee the results of violent attitudes on both sides. Such questions as war taxes and the draft would have to be faced again.

Woolman—the quiet schoolmaster, reflecting tailor, respected minister—followed the news with sorrow, but what is within a man always makes first call upon his attention, and as he read the papers, met with international merchants in Philadelphia, and attended discussion groups, he moved about mildly immune to it all. The schoolmaster was dwelling deep within himself in that year, with very few outward expressions of ministry to others. To his neighbors he appeared to have retired. But his soul had not yet found peace from the subtle dissatisfactions that had disturbed him for the last several years. The religious experience during his illness had comforted him deeply, but there must still be some responsibility to be faced.

By April his strength was restored, and the world of here and now commanded his attention and drew him out of himself; for his daughter and John Comfort had declared their intention to wed, and the wedding was to take place in the Mount Holly Meeting House. The ceremony would be as John's and Sarah's, and as Samuel's and Elizabeth's before them had been: plain, moving, significant, enduring.

It was another John's turn to quake, as he walked down the center aisle with Mary Woolman and saw Mary's parents and his parents and a host of relatives waiting in their places. The bride's father may have longed to see a son married, too; but John Comfort had won a close place in the Woolman family that almost compensated for the boy whose life had been so short.

After the wedding the bride and groom lived with John and Sarah temporarily, and during the spring and summer John Woolman planned a lavish wedding present for his daughter: a house on his own acres, built stoutly of brick. He found some temporary happiness in building, because while he was preoccupied with purchasing brick, nails, shingles, stones, lime, glass, hooks and hinges, window casings; while he was busy drawing plans, keeping scrupulous accounts of his expenditures, he was escaping for a little while from himself.

Escaping from himself into the happy task and the solving of his last problem overlapped. During the summer of 1771, when he was still busy supervising the building of Mary's house, a visiting Friends' minister from Dublin, Ireland, Samuel Neale, arrived at Rancocas. He had been traveling through the Carolinas and Virginia toward New Jersey, and after making the rounds of Meetings on the Atlantic seaboard he stopped at Trenton, Bordentown, and Upper Springfield, just north of Mount Holly.

Visiting Friends from abroad always caused a stir of interest, because they were usually talented speakers and they were full of news of the English towns and villages from which many of the colonists had come. Between Mansfield and Old Springfield Samuel Neale visited a Meeting called the "Neck," and the crowd that gathered to hear him was so large the Meeting had to be moved out under the trees.

That night he was the guest of Abner Woolman, but Samuel Neale really wanted to meet Abner's brother John. John Woolman enjoyed a wider reputation than he had any idea of on both sides of the ocean, and it was a disappointed traveler who returned home not having met John Woolman or heard him speak.

Samuel Neale saw John Woolman at Rancocas Meeting and found him to be "a sweet, clean-spirited Friend . . . of savoury conversation and pious self-denying life." At the Mount Holly Meeting the next day he not only saw him but talked with him and went home to dinner with him.

Neale, like so many of Woolman's contemporaries, saw in Woolman the rare and wonderful exception to humankind: the saint. Woolman was achieving a kind of sainthood without withdrawing from the world. His mission was with men, not away from them; his task was to share in and solve the problems of men.

From Samuel Neale John Woolman received a different kind of fillip—the nature of his next mission. After he had talked with his guest for a while, he knew that he must go to England. No terrible doubts, no reluctance to proceed, followed this inspiration. The direction was clear, and with a new exhilaration John Woolman told his family of his latest plan.

His wife heard the news with a kind of resignation she had found practical during the twenty-two years she had been married to John Woolman. His daughter and her brand new husband looked at each other anxiously; a war was brewing; hostile feelings were spreading.

"There is much of the slave trade in England," he said to them.

In England Friends could not hold public office because of their refusal to be members of or pay tithes to the Church of England, but they could, if sufficiently aroused, bring pressure to bear on those who were in legislative positions.

Sarah ventured one suggestion. "Winter is the time of bad weather on the Atlantic."

He nodded reassuringly.

"I shall wait until spring."

This was the Seventh Month, July, and he would have nearly a year to finish Mary's house, write his will that would appoint Stephen Comfort (John Comfort's father) as trustee over his properties, set all of his affairs in order, purchase items he would need for the voyage, and arrange ship passage.

"Beloved wife," he added, "do not worry too greatly."

23

LONDON

A sea voyage in the eighteenth century was never a pleasant prospect. Sailing ships were small and slow and uncomfortable at best. Their first concern was their cargo, and passengers had to provide food and bedding for themselves. Woolman was aware of the difficulties when he went to Philadelphia in the spring to book passage. He had heard them from other Friends.

He learned that Samuel Emlen had taken cabin space on the *Mary and Elizabeth,* a vessel with a Quaker owner. Samuel Emlen was the kind of companion Woolman liked: a scholar and a linguist, an experienced traveling minister who had already been to Great Britain and Ireland with Abraham Farrington. Samuel Emlen was a wealthy Philadelphian, and so he had engaged the more costly cabin space. Woolman wasn't poor; he could have done the same; but when he went aboard the *Mary and Elizabeth* to look her over, he experienced a "draught" in his mind and announced that he would travel steerage.

Emlen frankly wept.

"Please reconsider, John Woolman. Thou art not a strong and well man!"

Those words had been spoken to John Woolman so many times during his life that they had lost their meaning. "Reconsider!" the young men of the tavern had said. "Reconsider!" the disposers of slaves in their wills had pleaded. "Reconsider!" the ministers of his Meeting had begged when he proposed to risk his life among the Indians.

He and Emlen went down into the steerage and sat on a chest while sailors worked and bustled around them. Soon the ship's owner came down and invited them up to his own cabin. Woolman shook his head and announced,

"If I take passage with thee, it will be in the steerage."

Pleadings and reasonings of other Friends, including Israel Pemberton, did no good. Woolman had looked at the "superfluity of workmanship" in the cabin quarters and determined that his own money would not go to defray such unnecessary expenses. There was a deeper compulsion, too: the undying concern for his fellow men, the crew working and living below decks. When the *Mary and Elizabeth* left the dock at Philadelphia, she carried Emlen as a cabin passenger and John Woolman in steerage.

She carried a John Woolman whose heart yearned toward his family and whose soul was compelled toward duty. He had done everything he could to provide for his wife and daughter and son-in-law lest he not return; but the parting with Sarah had been difficult for them both. He earnestly wanted to come back to them, to walk into the house on Old Springfield Road once more, gather his wife and daughter into his arms, smell the preparation of his kind of food, and say, "It was a rewarding journey."

First the skyline of Philadelphia disappeared and then the shoreline of America. The homespun minister, headed for the sophisticated capital of Quakerism, sat alone on the deck and reflected.

The *Journal*, the literary treasure with which Woolman has endowed us, he had left with John Pemberton. There could possibly be some value in it, he had hoped humbly, and he would write further pages as he traveled.

"But I do not wish it published, except I should die abroad," he had said firmly.

He had put all his financial affairs into scrupulous order. He had written letters wherever he felt they were needed, and a long farewell epistle to the Quarterly and Monthly Meetings of Friends, full of love and faith and devotion.

"Where people are divinely gathered into a holy fellowship, and faithfully abide under the influence of that Spirit which leads into all Truth, these are they who are the light of the world," his epistle reminded them.

Aboard ship with Woolman were other Quaker passengers besides Emlen, all cabin occupants, and they could meet often on deck or in a cabin for conversation and worship. It was not they who took up Woolman's interest, though. His attention turned toward the seamen and their difficult life, and toward five Quaker lads he discovered among the crew.

"These boys bound as apprentices to learn seamanship need me," he explained to his companions wistfully. "So do the mature seamen."

The hard and pitiless life of the seamen gave Woolman a deep exercise. They saw the worst of life and were influenced by it. Many had shipped aboard slaving vessels and aboard ships of war. Their reaction to him was rough and hostile and full of roaring laughter—at first—but after a while the hardest of the hard men began to yield to his winning personality and to take kindly to him, and before many days some of the seamen were attending the Quaker Meetings in the cabin.

A voyage took a full month, and it was not all achieved in fair weather. A contrary sea with high waves and cold rain visited itself upon them during the first week, and as the tiny bark pitched and rolled, most of the passengers succumbed to wretched seasickness. Woolman indulged a secret little pride to discover himself a good sailor. "I have been preserved from sickness, my afflictions now being of another kind."

His affliction was still the lot of the seamen huddled in the steerage with him. They, of course, stood their watches around the clock since the ship sailed all night, and when they came down out of the rainy dark there wasn't enough room to hang up their wet clothing. Often their clothes were thrown in a heap on the floor where others walked over them.

Woolman tried to stay on deck as much as possible rather than add to their crowded condition, but during a high sea he had to go below. Then the hatch would have to be closed to keep out the water as the waves broke over the deck, and the air below became foul and dank. It wasn't hard for Woolman to imagine the lot of a captive slave, held in the steerage in chains for the entire voyage, badly fed if at all, never able to get up on deck, seasick, "heart loaded with grief." And it still went on!

A week of fair weather followed the storm, and passengers once more walked the decks, stomachs settled and spirits revived in the clear sea air. Woolman's recovery was a little slower, even though he hadn't been seasick. He had begun to experience difficulty breathing, and during the storm had

had to get up at night and put his mouth near a crack of the hatch to catch some air; but he felt "a reviving in his nature."

Crew and passengers lived through a second storm and came out of it into drizzle and fog.

"28th day, 5th month, 1772. Wet weather of late, small winds, dull sailing, inclining at times to calm. Our seamen have at several times cast a lead, and sounded I suppose about one hundred fathom but find no bottom. Foggy weather this morning."

They sounded bottom on the second day of the Sixth Month, and boyish excitement took hold of Woolman. It was no small thing to make a pilgrimage to the mother soil of Quakerism, to the land from which his own grandfather had migrated under William Penn's influence. England had been a kind of myth, a place from which visiting ministers came to America, a land far away out of which came remote political complications, and a place where Peter Andrews had died.

That same afternoon land was sighted, the tip of England, and by the fourth of June they were standing off Dover.

Samuel Emlen came and stood at Woolman's side near the rail. He was obviously dressed to go ashore.

"Thou art leaving?" Woolman asked.

"I am taking the stagecoach to London. Thou wouldst be wise to do the same."

Woolman hesitated. It distressed him deeply to part with his friend, but he replied,

"I feel I must stay aboard and sail all the way to London. The seamen need me. Our meetings have helped them."

The two men clasped hands and parted, to meet again at London.

On the seventh of June Woolman stood at the rail once more as the ship floated at anchor, waiting for a rising tide to take her up the Thames River. England seemed very flat at first glance, flat and marshy and green, and he had plenty of time to survey it because the trip up the narrow river swarming with small craft was slow and nerve-racking. The sailing vessel that had just negotiated an ocean seemed clumsy and awkward here. He was feeling frankly impatient. London Yearly Meeting was already in session! He wanted to be ashore!

Through a retreating fog the sprawling outline of London at last came into view, a long array of low buildings, their roofs full of round chimneys, and in the distance St. Paul's Cathedral dome. The ship passed the Tower of London before it docked, and Woolman wondered how William Penn had felt within its confines.

When at last the *Mary and Elizabeth* was tied to her dock, the anxious Woolman bade farewell to his friends in the crew and stepped ashore, pausing for nothing as he hastened toward Yearly Meeting. Heedless of himself or his surroundings, he strode through the narrow cobbled streets to the corner of Lombard and Gracechurch streets. A little pause before entering the Gracechurch Street Meeting; this had been William Penn's Meeting House.

John Woolman opened the door and stepped inside, saw the Meeting of Ministers and Elders already convened, and as quietly as possible walked to the table at the front of the room, handed the clerk his certificate, and sat down in the first available seat.

A deathly silence settled down around him.

That white hat! Those rumpled, dowdy, homespun, un-dyed clothes, even white stockings and shoes of untreated leather! The highest-ranking Friends in the world, and the most conservative, in their dull black beaver hats, their drab browns and blacks and grays, their expertly tailored coats and britches, stared unbelieving. Horrified, they sat completely stilled by the shocking scene.

The Philadelphia Friends had apparently recommended this visitor from the wilderness to "their Christian care!" And according to his certificate he wanted to tour England!

After a moment of bristling silence, a weighty Friend arose in place, cleared his throat, and with a touch of self-consciousness but with a clear understanding of his responsibility to Quakerdom, spoke. Perhaps the stranger from America could feel that his "dedication to this apprehended service was accepted and that without further labor he could return home."

John Woolman looked about him unbelieving, and the tears started in his eyes. These were Friends and fellows who were rejecting him. He had come so many thousands of miles on this mission of love, and he had come because he had a message to share with them. He had left home and family and had made a difficult sea voyage in spite of failing health. A pain shot through his heart, a sudden grief weighted him down, and he bowed his head for several minutes, replying only when he had recovered some of his equilibrium.

He did not feel himself released from his assignment, he told them as he rose to his feet, but he could not speak as a minister in the Friends' Meetings of England without the unity of the group. So, until such time as it appeared clear for him to go ahead, perhaps Friends would help him to find employment to support himself. He understood the mechanical trade.

They had heard the words of a true minister, and they knew it—words completely devoid of anger, spoken with a voice that had forgotten the meaning of recrimination years ago. The quality of the silence changed. After a period of meditation, John Woolman rose in place a second time, possessed by words given him to speak, granted the power and language as he had been at his own Yearly Meeting when it became his responsibility to move men's hearts, and a lifetime of experience went into his sermon.

When he finished and eased his frame gently down into his seat once more, the Friend who had invited him to return to America a mere quarter of an hour earlier arose slowly, covered with humility. He wished to admit his error, to withdraw his suggestion, he said, and to declare himself in complete unity with the visiting American.

A little wave of happy relief rippled over the room, and at the rise of the Meeting hands were extended to John Woolman from every side. He was a Friend among Friends, a brother from across the sea, beloved, accepted, at one with them, and he was free to join in the fellowship of the Yearly Meeting and to go on from there to his tour of England.

London Yearly Meeting gathered immediately afterward in the same historic Meeting House on Gracechurch Street, and it was ready to hear John Woolman's message. For years Yearly Meeting epistles had been exchanged between London and Philadelphia. Many of the Philadelphia epistles written by committees on which John Woolman had served were signed by a long list of weighty Friends that often included John Woolman's name. London Friends visiting America had heard John Woolman speak in his own Meeting.

John Woolman spoke to London Friends on slavery. Slavery in England was not so much an adjunct of a one-crop economy that required hand labor; it was an industry in its own right, an industry in which England was the leader with control of at least half the slave trade of the world by John Woolman's time. There were nearly two hundred British slavers plying the high seas, able to carry a total of 50,000 slaves. Often merchants brought home their personal slaves. Slave auctions were advertised in the English papers, and runaway slaves were sought.

The London Yearly Meeting had recorded a minute as far back as 1727 against the "importation of Negroes from their native country and relations"; in 1758 (Philadelphia's great year) the subject appeared on London records again—in the official epistle that went out to Quarterly and Monthly Meetings of Great Britain, Ireland, and elsewhere. Three years later London followed Philadelphia's example and decided to disown Friends who were concerned in the "unchristian traffic." When John Woolman finished speaking, they found they wanted to record a further minute on slavery, and eleven years after his visit they would petition Parliament to outlaw the practice.

Woolman went home that evening and after each subsequent day's sessions with John Townsend, a well-to-do dealer in pewterware, who often entertained traveling Friends. He went home with him through streets that he found crowded and busy, full of constant traffic, people on horseback, in carriages, on foot, through streets that were not laid out with anything like the regularity and plan of Philadelphia's streets. London seemed to be full of small tradesmen; so many of the houses had signs hanging out front: "Children educated here," "Shoes mended here," or "Funerals furnished here." London had many more Friends Meeting Houses, and Woolman hoped to see at least some of them. Not far from Gracechurch Street Meeting was Devonshire House, and just out of Aldersgate Street had been the Bull and Mouth, oldest of them all.

"Dear Wife," he wrote home from London, "The tender

concern which I have many times felt for thee and for Mary and John . . . I may not easily express. I have often remembered you with tears . . ."

To cousins he wrote, "I am middling well in London, and believe I may go northward in a few days."

He was really anxious to get on with his pilgrimage, to walk through the English countryside, perhaps visit Gloucestershire, where the Woolman family had originated, and Leicestershire, where George Fox was born, and journey up into Lancashire, Westmoreland, and Yorkshire, where George Fox had traveled and preached with such amazing success.

He was ready to visit this kingdom of George Fox and to do his humble share toward the "establishment of Friends in the pure life of Truth."

24

GEORGE FOX'S KINGDOM

Woolman bade his London associates farewell and set out northward to the town of Hertford, where he attended a Quarterly Meeting. Then his trudging took him westward into the Oxfordshire country, with its rolling hills and meadowy land, its thick woods and country estates. English countryside, he was discovering, was quite different from the American wilderness. England was steeped in history, with some of its roads so ancient they had been built by the Romans. He liked the milestones that he passed at regular intervals. They were encouraging, as each stone told him how many miles he had covered and how many remained before he should reach his next destination, next Meeting, next hospitable Quaker home.

He tried to visit every Meeting as he turned northward again toward Northampton, the shoe manufacturing city, and Banbury, trudging along until he became weary, resting beside the road to recover his strength, always driven on by the need to share his convictions with others and to achieve perfect peace within himself.

"17th day: 7th month: was this day at Birmingham; I have been at meetings at Coventry, at Warwick, in Oxford-shire, and sundry places, and have felt the humbling hand of the Lord upon me; but through his tender mercies I find peace in the labours I have gone through."

The humbling hand of the Lord was extreme fatigue. Each morning he started out a little more stiffly than the day before. Woolman was more tired and spent than he dared ad-mit to himself, but he must complete his journey.

Birmingham was big, noisy, boisterous, teeming with thou-sands of the "world's people." Alehouses were more pros-perous than coffeehouses; traders were full of trickery; money counterfeiters abounded. Birmingham was a manu-facturing town that made items of steel and iron: locks, hinges, metal buttons, nails, and screws, and before the days of mass production much of the manufacturing was done by hand in the cottages of the workers at incredibly low wages.

Woolman found the Meeting House on upper Bull Street that was part of the main street through town. Streets changed their names every few blocks in the eighteenth cen-tury, because the houses had no numbers. There were not many Quakers here, but they made a stanch group that had been meeting for worship since 1682.

On past another manufacturing town and out into the agri-cultural regions once more, still amazed by the beautiful hilly countryside, his farmer's eye always noting the health of a flock of sheep that was being driven along the same road, or the progress of a stand of wheat. He passed thatched roofed cottages and small farms, sometimes stopping for a drink of water.

"Why dost thou walk?" Friends asked him often. "There is a stagecoach."

He walked because his views on slavery were all-inclusive. He had observed the stagecoaches with their six horses as they galloped and clattered by, sacrificing all human considerations for speed. They rode hard without stopping, sometimes covering a hundred miles in twenty-four hours, sometimes driving the horses to death. The boys who rode on top of the coaches or astride the lead horses were said to freeze to death at their posts in bad weather.

No, thank you! That was not something in which John Woolman cared to participate. He did not even want any mail to be delivered to him by these posts.

English people (Friends among them) were mixed up with slavery in subtle ways. They drew profit from the trade; they dealt in the fruits of slave labor; they used superfluities in dress and in their homes which indirectly aided the need for more slave labor; they enslaved one another with low wages; and they enslaved post boys to achieve nerve-racking and unnecessary speed.

Woolman walked—day after day and week after week. By the time he came out onto a rise of ground and gazed ahead of him at the city of Nottingham, it was the end of July.

Nottingham was another populous manufacturing city, noted for its laces, where the streets were narrow and the sidewalks narrower and the houses two or three stories high. The city lay along the River Trent and bristled with windmills. Nottingham had a special meaning for John Woolman, because it was there that George Fox had been arrested for the first time and cast into the jail for preaching religious doctrine that was contrary to the laws of England.

Woolman walked northward again from Nottingham through wild, unspoiled country—moors covered with heather and waist-high forests of gorse and bracken, flocks of sheep grazing on hillsides—to Sheffield, noted for its silver plate and cutlery.

If he continued approximately northward he would come to York, his ultimate goal, but before he did that he had something else in mind: the lake country in the northwest. So he turned from Sheffield toward Preston Patrick, Settle, and Kendal. Names that had been meaningful, promising words in George Fox's *Journal* throughout John Woolman's life were now becoming real. George Fox had traveled along these same roads sowing his precious seed, and wherever a seed had fallen a Meeting had sprung up.

The scenery grew wilder and craggier as he approached Kendal; high fells and glens, valleys and lakes marked the land, and in the background were towering hills. He passed tiny hamlets and now and again a lonely cottage, white-washed and thatched, until at last, weary to the point of collapse, he looked down at old, drab-colored Kendal in the valley of the Kent. The sight dissolved his fatigue and he hurried along the road.

The road he was walking led directly into town, crossing a bridge over the River Kent into the street called Stramongate on which stood the Friends' Meeting House. It was among the oldest Friends' Meeting Houses in England; over its door were carved the numbers 1688.

The Wilson family entertained him in Kendal, flung open the door of their opulent home to the dusty, weary, odd-looking minister, gave him an opportunity to bathe and rest and launder his linens.

"Wilt thou stay with us until thou art rested?" Isaac Wilson asked.

"I should like to remain with thee for a while, but I must go on to York."

Rachel Wilson was a minister herself and had visited America three years earlier, and she had delivered a sermon in Philadelphia that had touched deeply upon Woolman's indecision about his trip to the West Indies. He had looked forward to a talk with her, but she was away on another visiting-minister journey. So he passed his time with her husband Isaac and her children.

The Wilsons belonged to the wealthy few in Kendal who made their wealth from the hand laborers of the weaving industry, the villagers who spun and wove wool and cotton in their cottages. As he became acquainted with the city of Kendal, Woolman had to realize that thousands were constantly employed as a result of the management of such families as the Wilsons, but he was disturbed that the Wilsons had so much of the world's goods in their home.

John Woolman left Kendal the end of August and headed eastward toward York, a distance of about ninety English miles. His pace was slowing; the roads grew longer, the dust dustier; the end of summer brought more rainy days, chill and penetrating. If only he had been granted the physique and endurance of George Fox! He had none of the imprisonments and other hardships to face that had lain in Fox's path. He rarely had to lie out in the open at night. He could travel from one hospitable Quaker home to another. Yet his strength was flagging.

He drove himself on and promised himself that he could have an adequate rest at York before beginning the return journey to London.

"6th day: 9th month: and first of the week. I was this day at Counterside, a large Meeting House and very full. Through the opening of pure love, it was a strengthening time to me, and I believe to many more."

"13th day: 9th month: This day I was at Leyburn, a small Meeting; but, the townspeople coming in, the house was crowded."

Autumn. Woolman traveled "often in wet weather and through narrow streets in towns and villages where was dirtiness under foot and the scent arising from that filth which more or less infects the air of all thick and settled towns was disagreeable."

A note of comfort came out of the atmosphere of the dirty towns: there could be no difficulty about knowing when undyed clothing was clean. It was a thought come lately, but it comforted John Woolman, who had not really forgotten the embarrassment he had suffered in Yearly Meeting. Dyes, he reasoned, were invented partly to please the eye, and partly to hide dirt. If all the money that people spent on dyestuffs were applied to keeping sweet and clean, how much cleaner people would be!

He began to leave the hills behind him as he approached the York region. The land flattened out to sea level—meadow country for oats and potatoes—and he could see the city miles ahead, the minster (cathedral) towering above the skyline. York stood out white against the green country, because the ancient walls that surrounded it were built of the white limestone from nearby Tadcaster.

Woolman sat down beside the road to rest his body and collect his thoughts. He longed for the comfort and hospitality that he knew would be his in York, but the minister must bring something with him, too.

He had seen so much, experienced so much, felt so deeply

on so many new subjects, that he needed to pause before entering upon this stronghold of Quakerism, this city where George Fox had first come in 1651 to enter the minster itself and challenge the priests. Fox had visited York again and again, to be set upon by mobs, to preach, to convince so many of the highborn and low.

Woolman had seen the condition of the poor, "some of whom though honest and industrious, have nothing to spare toward paying for the schooling of their children." He had seen the wealthy laying up treasure. He had walked over the rich spiritual earth out of which the Society of Friends had grown and had sat in worship time and again with Fox's "Children of Light." He had been moved to give messages often, messages that pointed out the miseries produced by the slave trade, the distresses of dealing in superfluities, and the beauty and significance of silent worship. In his travels he had met Friends who had lost touch with their own faith, who knew little of the nature of silent worship, and to these he had spoken fervently.

If Friends understand their own faith, he concluded, if they live it and share it with the rest of mankind, their "lives will have an inviting language."

John Woolman struggled up from a sitting position. His joints ached, his muscles were lame, his feet burned; but he smiled as he looked down the road that curved gently toward York and the River Ouse.

When the last milestone appeared by the roadside, Woolman saw the figure of a man walking toward him. The figure was younger, more vigorous, not at all tired or bent as he felt. The eighteen-year-old hurried toward Woolman and held out his hand.

"Thou art John Woolman!"

He was Henry Tuke, he explained, and he had come out

to escort the minister to his home. His mother, Esther Tuke, had met Woolman in London. Letters had preceded him to York, and York Friends were all excited about him. Henry Tuke's animation at being the first to meet John Woolman and to walk beside him and talk to him was apparent in the boy's eyes and face. Later Henry described his company as indescribably sweet. He took the older man's bundle and slowed his own eager pace.

Gracious and lovely Esther Tuke was at the door with her hand outstretched to greet the illustrious visitor.

"We have expected thee for so long, John Woolman!"

"I am glad to see thee again, Esther Tuke."

"My husband is anxious to meet thee, too."

The Tukes owned an ample house on Castlegate, but there were a lot of Tukes—William and Esther and seven children —and they filled the house. To them were added the neighbors who dropped in to meet John Woolman. John Woolman found in their home a kind of happy commotion like that he had once known in the old Rancocas farmhouse of his father. He allowed himself to be swept into the circle and into the activities of the Quaker community without protest. A good meal, a bath, fresh linen, a night's sleep would restore him.

But when he awoke the next morning, the twenty-third of September, one night's rest had not been enough, and two nights were not going to suffice either. The all-night bustle of the city streets was not for him, nor was its tainted air; and the Tuke children had risen with the dawn.

Too thoughtful to complain, he went to York Quarterly Meeting with the family, sustained himself as best he could through the long Meeting, spoke on the subject of slavery, and walked home again with the Tukes, sinking into a chair the minute he was in the house.

"Thou art tired!" Esther Tuke exclaimed.

They hovered around him lovingly. He had traveled too many miles in too short a time! He must stay with them a long while, until he was completely rested.

With real embarrassment John Woolman knew what he must do to recover his health and strength fully: he must escape from the hubbub of the Tuke household. They were Friends. Why should he not trust them to understand such a need? He did trust them, and they did understand.

"I am accustomed to sleeping in the clean quiet countryside and in a house not so full of happy folk as thine."

The Tukes arranged immediately for Woolman to move to Almery Garth.

Almery Garth was a great old three-story house, full of big rooms, and occupied by a small family. It stood outside the city walls in the open fields, surrounded by gardens and lawns, in a street called Marygate, on land that had once belonged to the Abbey of St. Mary's. The Priestmans, who owned Almery Garth, were close friends of the Tukes, and so it was easy to transfer the visitor from one side of the city to the other.

Thomas Priestman eagerly led Woolman to his best-appointed guest room, but Woolman shook his head as he gazed at its appointments.

"Dost thou have a smaller, plainer one?"

Thomas Priestman told him to choose any room in the house, and after inspecting several John Woolman selected one of the smaller rooms, with whitewashed walls, no hanging ornaments, a plain oak fireplace, and two beds hung with undyed linens. Its window looked out from the side of the house, and come morning John Woolman would be able to lean out and look over the meadows to the River Ouse in the distance.

The Priestmans understood, as did the Tukes, that John Woolman wanted to spend several days in bed, and so they all left him, the Tukes returning to Castlegate and the Priestmans cautioning their children to take their noise to another floor.

Woolman closed the door gently on all the solicitude and moved across the room, taking hold of the back of a chair to steady himself as a feeling of dizziness swept over him. His face was hot, his stomach nauseous. The Tukes were right; he really had overtaxed himself.

He looked at the inviting bed that awaited him and managed not to yield to the desire to retire at once. There were one or two letters . . . some of his belongings . . . "Beloved Cousins: I am now at York at a Quarterly Meeting 23 day: 9 month: '72 . . . I often remember you and friends in your parts as I pass along this journey . . . I left my bed and some things on board the ship I came in directing the people to convey them to you if they arrive safe at Philadelphia. John Woolman."

He laid down the quill. Other letters would have to wait, he realized, because he had reached a point of absolute fatigue.

Removing his clothes, he slid between the fresh sheets and lay still, waiting for his pulse to subside. The dizzy sensation seemed like the motion of a ship when he lay flat. He did manage to sleep fitfully, haunted by fragments of dreams and garbled memories, but the next morning he found it impossible to rise. He spent the next four days in bed, resting and dozing, and the Priestmans never disturbed him except to bring food. The food he rarely ate, because his head still burned and his appetite had vanished, his pulse raced, and his back ached.

On the morning of the fifth day, Thomas Priestman came

into John Woolman's room, bent over him, and gave him only one glance. Then he went out, mounted his horse, and rode to the Tukes'.

"John Woolman," he told them, "John Woolman"—and his voice quavered—"has the smallpox."

It was First Day, but Esther Tuke did not go to Meeting that morning. She returned to Almery Garth with Thomas Priestman and went straight to the sickroom.

Esther Tuke was noted for her beauty, and in a century when smallpox marred the loveliest of women she was conspicuously beautiful because she had never contracted the disease. Without a flicker of hesitation she entered John Woolman's room, removed her cloak and hood, and took the sick man's hand in hers.

"Friend," she whispered gently, and Woolman opened his eyes.

He closed his eyes again, and she knew that he knew. There could be no thought of keeping from him the nature of his affliction, because he had himself administered to the sick in Rancocas and Mount Holly. He had watched his own sister die of the horrible disease.

Not everyone died of smallpox. The Tukes and Priestmans hoped for Woolman's recovery during the first few days, because of his great moral strength if for no other reason.

John Woolman thought of the trouble he was causing so many people, and he asked for as little as possible.

"Wilt thou have a doctor?" they asked him.

"I have not liberty in my mind to do so," he replied.

But a young man, not of the Society, who was an apothecary came anyway of his own accord. He and Woolman consulted together about the treatment.

The next day Woolman's mind seemed affected for a while, and realizing it he asked that nothing be given him against which he had any scruple. Later that day he asked someone to take down his thoughts, and he broke forth into prayer.

Esther Tuke, William Tuke, the Priestmans, all took their turns at his side to render every possible comfort and service, day and night. When he awoke on the morning of the third day he said, "I don't know that I have slept this night. I feel the disorder making its progress; but my mind is mercifully preserved in stillness and peace."

And when he began to realize that he could not recover, his thoughts turned to his family. "Though I feel them near to me at this time, yet I have freely given them up."

As the disease followed its inevitable course, he became more dependent upon the presence of Esther Tuke.

"Please do not sleep out of the house until you see an alteration in my condition."

She promised to remain.

Sarah Tuke, Esther's eighteen-year-old daughter, came at night so that her mother could get a few hours' sleep; and as she sat by his bedside John Woolman spoke to her,

"My child, thou seemst very kind to me, a poor creature. The Lord will reward thee for it."

As symptoms followed one upon another—the swollen, fluid-filled eruptions, the fever, the dry and cracked lips, the sore throat, the failing eyesight—Woolman's mind remained clear. Although he could hardly see and had scarcely enough strength to lift his hand, he asked from time to time for pen and paper to write down fragments of thoughts, or he dictated sentences that he wanted added to his *Journal*. He even gave detailed instructions for his own burial:

"An ash coffin made plain without any manner of superfluities, the corpse to be wrapped in cheap flannel, the expense of which I leave my wearing clothes to defray. . . ."

By the end of a week his throat had almost completely

closed up, and the doctor syringed it so that he could swallow. Lying flat on his back became unbearable, and Woolman whispered to them to lift him up to a chair. Fearfully, two Friends supported him as he rose from the bed and eased him into the chair. Esther Tuke hastened to fold a blanket around his knees. His voice was almost gone, his eyes almost blind, but he wanted to write once more, a last message, and so they brought him pen and ink.

"I believe my being here is in the wisdom of Christ," he wrote. "I know not as to life or death."

Completely spent by the effort, he had to be supported back to the bed, where he sank down and closed his eyes.

"About a quarter before six the same morning [October 7] he seemed to fall into an easy sleep, which continued about half an hour; when seeming to awake, he breathed a few times with a little more difficulty, and so expired without a sign, groan or struggle." So reported William Tuke.

Their own eyes blinded with tears, the Yorkshire Friends sat down to write letters to Sarah, to other Friends in America, to London, to any and all who would want to know of John Woolman's passing, and their name was legion. They laid him to rest in the Friends' graveyard in Bishophill, York, without even the vanity of a stone to mark the place, and two days after his death the Yorkshire Friends held a memorial Meeting for Worship in his name.

"He was a man endued with a large natural capacity," said the testimony of the Yorkshire Friends. "And being obedient to the manifestations of Divine Grace, having in patience and humility endured many deep baptisms, he became thereby sanctified and fitted for the Lord's work, and was truly serviceable in his church."

John Woolman was indeed a man endowed with large natural capacities, far beyond the capacities of other men, and his life was itself a living testimony to a living faith. He believed as the Friends believe, that God can speak to any man and that God can speak through him to other men. John Woolman surrendered himself to being a trumpet to sound forth His language.

Because his spiritual ear was so sensitive to divine message, and because his insight was so keen, he understood that most of the sufferings of mankind are caused by greed. If men did not want more than their share of the world's goods there would be no wars. If men did not want more than enough of comforts they would not be tempted to enslave one another.

Shedding light upon the evils of slavery was Woolman's greatest contribution to mankind, but it was not his final goal. He sought a closer personal harmony with God, and his testimony against slavery was a rich fruit of that saintly search. John Woolman's greatest mission in life was wooing the beauty of God and sharing that beauty with his fellow men.

BIBLIOGRAPHY

ATWATER, MARY MEIGS. *The Shuttle-Craft Book of American Hand-Weaving.* New York: 1951.

BANCROFT, GEORGE. *History of the United States of America.* New York: 1888.

BARLOW, ALFRED. *The History and Principles of Weaving.* London: 1879.

BARBER, JOHN W. AND HENRY HOWE. *Historical Collections of the State of New Jersey.* New York: 1845.

BECK, HENRY CHARLTON. *Fare to Midlands, Forgotten Towns of Central New Jersey.* New York: 1939.

BENEZET, ANTHONY. *A Short Account of the People Called Quakers.* Philadelphia: 1758.

BENTON, JOHN. "The John Woolman Memorial." (Unpublished paper.)

BENTON, JOSEPHINE M. "John Woolman, Most Modern of Ancient Friends." Philadelphia: 1952. (Pamphlet.)

BLOUNT, MRS. GODFREY. *The Story of Homespun Web.* London (no date).

BOWNE, SAMUEL. "History of Mount Holly Meeting House." (Unpublished paper.)

BRAITHWAITE, WILLIAM C. *The Beginnings of Quakerism.* London: 1923.

———. *The Second Period of Quakerism.* London: 1919.

BRIDENBAUGH, CARL. *Cities in the Wilderness.* New York: 1938.

BRINTON, DANIEL G. *The Lenape and Their Legends.* Philadelphia: 1885.

BRINTON, HOWARD. *Friends for 300 Years.* New York: 1952.

CHURCHMAN, JOHN. *An Account of the Gospel Labours, and Christian Experiences of a Faithful Minister of Christ.* Philadelphia: 1779.

CLARKSON, THOMAS. *A Portraiture of Quakerism.* New York: 1806.

COOPER, HOWARD M. *Historical Sketch of Camden.* Camden: 1931.

COUPLAND, REGINALD. *The British Anti-Slavery Movement.* London: 1933.

CROSS, DOROTHY. "The Indians of New Jersey." (Pamphlet) 1939.

DENT, ROBERT K. *Old and New Birmingham.* Birmingham: 1880.

DE COU, GEORGE. *Moorestown and Her Neighbors.* Philadelphia: 1929.

———. "Historical Sketches of Rancocas and Neighborhood." (Pamphlet) 1937.

———. *Burlington, a Provincial Capital.* Philadelphia: 1945.

DOUGLAS-LITHGOW, R. A. *Nantucket, a History*. New York: 1914.

DRAKE, THOMAS. E. *Quakers and Slavery in America*. New Haven: 1950.

DUNLAP, WILLIAM C. *Quaker Education in Baltimore and Virginia Yearly Meetings*. Philadelphia: 1936.

ENGLISH GENTLEMAN, BY AN. *A Tour in England and Scotland in 1785*. London: 1788.

FOTHERGILL, SAMUEL. *Memoirs of the Life and Gospel Labours of Samuel Fothergill* . . . London: 1857.

GILBERT, DOROTHY LLOYD. "First Friends at New Garden in North Carolina." (Pamphlet.) (Reprint from the Autumn Number, 1945, of the *Bulletin of Friends Historical Association*.)

GRAY, DUNCAN. *Nottingham through 500 Years*. Nottingham: 1949.

GREEN, JOHN RICHARD. *A Short History of the English People*. London: 1900.

GUMMERE, AMELIA MOTT. *The Quaker, a Study in Costume*. Philadelphia: 1901.

———. *The Journal and Essays of John Woolman*. Philadelphia: 1922.

HARGROVE, WILLIAM. *History and Description of the City of York*. York: 1818.

HAYNES, GEORGE F. "John Woolman and the Coming Age." *Friends Intelligencer*. Eighth Month 17, 1946.

HAZARD, CAROLINE. *The Narragansett Friends' Meeting in the XVIII Century*. Boston: 1899.

———. *Thomas Hazard Son of Robert, called College Tom*. Boston: 1893.

HOLMES, MRS. BASIL. "Haunts of the London Quakers." *The Antiquary*, January, 1899.

JANNEY, SAMUEL M. *The Life of William Penn*. Philadelphia: 1871.

JONES, RUFUS M. "Evidences of the Influence of Quietism on John Woolman." *Friends Intelligencer*. Third Month 6, 1948.

———. *The Quakers in the American Colonies*. London: 1923.

JORNS, AUGUSTE. *The Quakers as Pioneers in Social Work*. New York: 1931.

KELSEY, RAYNER WICKERSHAM. *Friends and the Indians 1655–1917*. Philadelphia: 1917.

KNIGHT, CHARLES BRUNTON. *A History of the City of York*. London: 1944.

LEADER, ROBERT EADON. *Reminiscences of Old Sheffield*. Sheffield: 1876.

London Yearly Meeting During 250 Years. London: 1919.

LOWRY, ANN GIDLEY. "The Story of the Flushing Meeting House." (Pamphlet). Flushing: 1939.

MACLEANE, LAUCHLIN. An Essay on the Expediency of Inoculation. Philadelphia: 1756.

MICHENER, EZRA. A Retrospect of Early Quakerism. Philadelphia: 1860.

MORGAN, GEORGE. The City of Firsts. Philadelphia: 1926.

MORITZ, C. P. Travels in England in 1782. New York: 1885.

NEALE, SAMUEL. Life and Religious Labors of Samuel Neale. Philadelphia: 1847.

OSGOOD, HERBERT L. The American Colonies in the Eighteenth Century. New York: 1924.

PARRISH, SAMUEL. "Some Chapters in the History of the Friendly Association for Regaining and Preserving Peace with the Indians by Pacific Measures." (Pamphlet) Philadelphia: 1877.

PECKHAM, HOWARD H. Pontiac and the Indian Uprising. Princeton: 1947.

The Pennsylvania Gazette, Containing the Freshest Advices Foreign and Domestick. Selected issues from 1729 to 1760.

PENNYPACKER, ISAAC R. "The Old Tavern at Haddonfield." (Pamphlet) Haddonfield: 1901.

PROUD, ROBERT. The History of Pennsylvania in North America. Philadelphia: 1797.

RUSH, BENJAMIN. "Inoculating for the Small-Pox." (Appendix of Medical Inquiries and Observations.) Philadelphia: 1789.

RUSSELL, ELBERT. The History of Quakerism. New York: 1942.

SHAW, CHARLES. A Topographical and Historical Description of Boston. Boston: 1817.

SHORE, W. TEIGNMOUTH. John Woolman, His Life and Our Times. London: 1913.

SMITH, SAMUEL. The History of the Colony of Nova-Caesaria, or New-Jersey. Burlington: 1765.

SOCIETY OF FRIENDS: Department of Records, 302 Arch Street, Philadelphia, Pa.
 Minutes of the Yearly Meeting for Pennsylvania and New Jersey from 1706 to 1771.
 Minutes of the Meeting for Sufferings for Pennsylvania and New Jersey from 1756 to 1772 (selected).
 Minutes of the Burlington Men's Monthly Meeting 1678 to 1770.

SOCIETY OF FRIENDS: Friends Historical Library of Swarthmore College.

Original manuscripts of John Woolman's *Journal* 1720 to 1747, 1720 to 1770 (partly rewritten by him), and the English *Journal* from January to July, 1772. Original manuscripts of some of his essays. Microfilm records of minutes of Westbury Monthly Meeting, Virginia Yearly Meeting, Rhode Island Meeting, and Flushing Monthly Meeting (selected).

THAYER, THEODORE. *Israel Pemberton, King of the Quakers.* Philadelphia: 1943.

———. "The Friendly Association." *The Pennsylvania Magazine of History and Biography,* October, 1943.

THOMAS, ANNA BRAITHWAITE. *The Story of the Baltimore Yearly Meeting from 1672 to 1938.* Baltimore: 1938.

TOLLES, FREDERICK B. *Meeting House and Counting House.* Chapel Hill: 1948.

VAUX, ROBERTS. *Memoirs of the Life of Anthony Benezet.* Philadelphia: 1817.

———. *Memoirs of the Lives of Benjamin Lay and Ralph Sandiford.* Philadelphia: 1815.

WALLACE, ANTHONY F. *King of the Delawares: Teedyuscung.* Philadelphia: 1949.

WEEKS, STEPHEN B. *Southern Quakers and Slavery.* Baltimore: 1896.

WHELLAN, WILLIAM (editor). *The History and Topography of the Counties of Cumberland and Westmoreland.* London: 1860.

WHITEHEAD, WILLIAM A. *Contributions to the Early History of Perth Amboy and Adjoining Country.* New York: 1856.

WHITNEY, JANET. "Thoughts on the 175th Anniversary of John Woolman." *The Friend,* Tenth Month 9, 1947.

———. *John Woolman, American Quaker.* Boston: 1942.

WHITNEY, JANET (editor). *The Journal of John Woolman.* Chicago: 1950.

WHITTIER, JOHN GREENLEAF (editor). *The Journal of John Woolman.* Boston: 1871.

YOUNG, ARTHUR. *A Six Months Tour through the North of England.* London: 1770.